Since graduating from St Andrews University in history in 1970, Elspeth Wills has spent her career as a researcher, interpreter and writer within advertising, marketing, economic development and visitor attraction environments. She has written more than a dozen books on subjects as varied as natural history, new town development and Scottish innovation.

ABBOTSFORD TO ZION

THE STORY OF SCOTTISH PLACE NAMES AROUND THE WORLD

ELSPETH WILLS

To Fr[...]*e idea of*

First published in 2016 by
Birlinn Limited
West Newington House
10 Newington Road
Edinburgh
EH9 1QS

www.birlinn.co.uk

ISBN 978 1 78027 407 2

British Library Cataloguing-in-Publication Data
A catalogue record for this book is available from the British Library

Typeset by Initial Typesetting Services, Edinburgh
Printed and bound by Grafica Veneta (www.graficaveneta.com)

Contents

List of maps

Acknowledgements

Thanks go to the many friends and colleagues who have suggested names, often from personal experience. I am particularly grateful to Julian Crowe and Graeme Munro who read part of the manuscript and encouraged me to continue at a time when I was unsure whether the project merited a book. Graeme also undertook the time-consuming and tedious task of marking up potential names on a world atlas.

Introduction

Putting Scotland on the map

There is an old saying: 'Thaim wi a guid Scots tongue in their heid are fit tae gang ower the warld'. From Abbotsford in British Columbia to Zion in Illinois, Scots have made their mark on the world atlas either in naming places or having places named after them. It is even claimed that across the USA, Canada, the Caribbean, Australia, New Zealand, South Africa and Zimbabwe there is one Scottish place name for every four of English origin. There are at least 550 towns, suburbs, villages, mountains, rivers and other topographical features in South Africa alone with Scottish names, Johannesburg having one of the world's largest suburban clusters from Blairgowrie to Birnam. The density of Scottish place names relates closely to where Scots chose to settle, from Canadian provinces such as Ontario and Nova Scotia to Tasmania and New Zealand's South Island.

To list all the locations in the world named by or after Scots would read like the index of an atlas. There would be thousands of entries with names such as Balmoral or Braemar appearing in several continents and, in this case, chosen for the same reason, of honouring Queen Victoria's holiday haunt in the Highlands. *Abbotsford to Zion* seeks rather to tell the fascinating and occasionally bizarre stories behind a selection of these names.

In 1882 MP Sir Charles Dilke observed, 'In British settlements, from Canada to Ceylon, from Dunedin to Bombay, for

Aberdeen
Aberdour, Fife
Aberfoyle, Stirlingshire
Ailsa Craig, Ayrshire
Airdrie, Lanarkshire
Annandale, Dumfriesshire
Armadale, Skye
Arnprior, Stirlingshire
Arran, Ayrshire
Arthur's Seat, Edinburgh
Atholl, Perthshire
Aviemore, Inverness-shire
Avon river, Lanarkshire
Baldoon, Wigtownshire
Balmoral, Aberdeenshire
Banff, Banffshire
Bannockburn, Stirlingshire
Barra, Western Isles
Ben Lomond, Stirlingshire
Birsay, Orkney
Blair Atholl, Perthshire
Blantyre, Lanarkshire
Braemar, Aberdeenshire
Breadalbane, Perthshire
Calgary, Mull, Argyllshire
Callander, Stirlingshire
Carrick, Ayrshire
Cessnock, Ayrshire
Clyde river, Lanarkshire
Craigellachie, Moray
Cullen, Banffshire
Culloden, Inverness-shire
Culross, Fife
Dalhousie, Midlothian
Dalvey, Moray
Douglas, Lanarkshire
Dumbarton, Dunbartonshire
Dumfries, Dumfriesshire
Dunbar, East Lothian
Dunblane, Perthshire
Dundee
Dundonald, Ayrshire
Dunkeld, Perthshire

Dunsinane, Perthshire
Dunvegan, Skye,
  Inverness-shire
Edenglassie, Banffshire
Edinburgh
Elderslie, Renfrewshire
Elgin, Moray
Eskdale, Dumfriesshire
Firth of Tay, Angus/Fife
Fort William, Inverness-shire
Garry river, Inverness-shire
Glasgow
Glencoe, Inverness-shire
Gleneagles, Perthshire
Glenelg, Ross and Cromarty
Glengarry, Inverness-shire
Glenorchy, Argyllshire
Goatfell, Arran, Ayrshire
Grampian mountains,
  Aberdeenshire
Granton, Edinburgh
Greenock, Renfrewshire
Gretna, Dumfriesshire
Inverbervie, Aberdeenshire
Iona, Argyllshire
Islay, Argyllshire
Jura, Argyllshire
Kildonan, Sutherland
Kincardine, Fife
Kinloss, Moray
Kinross, Kinross-shire
Kintail, Ross and Cromarty
Kirkoswald, Ayrshire
Knapdale, Argyllshire
Lammermuir Hills,
  Midlothian
Leith, Edinburgh
Liddesdale, Roxburghshire
Loch Lomond, Stirlingshire
Loch Quoich, Inverness-shire
Lochalsh, Inverness-shire
Lochboisdale, South Uist,
  Western Isles

Lochinvar, Dumfriesshire
Lochleven, Kinross-shire
Lochnagar, Aberdeenshire
MacDuff, Banffshire
Mavisbank, Midlothian
Melrose, Roxburghshire
Melsetter, Orkney
Monklands, Lanarkshire
Monnymusk, Aberdeenshire
Montrose, Angus
Morar, Inverness-shire
Morvern, Argyllshire
Newburgh, Fife
North Esk river, Angus
Oban, Argyllshire
Orkney Islands
Perth
Portree, Skye, Inverness-shire
Renfrew, Renfrewshire
Riccarton, Ayrshire
Rothesay, Bute, Argyllshire
Roxburgh, Roxburghshire
Rutherglen, Lanarkshire
Sanquhar, Dumfriesshire
Scone, Perthshire
Shetland Islands
Skipness, Argyllshire
Solway Firth, Dumfriesshire
South Esk river, Angus
St Andrews, Fife
Strathmore, Perthshire
Strathspey, Inverness-shire
Stromness, Orkney
Tay river, Angus/Perthshire
Thrumster, Caithness
Tillicoultry,
  Clackmannanshire
Tobermory, Mull, Argyllshire
Tweed river, Roxburghshire
Ulva, Mull, Argyllshire
Urie river, Aberdeenshire
Ythan, Aberdeenshire

From Gretna Green to Shetland, Scots took their place names with them when settling abroad. The reasons for choosing the name varied: some wanted to remember their birthplace or the homelands of their ancestors, while others were reminded of similarities between new landscapes and those of home. Others were romantics . . . or simply homesick.

every Englishman that you meet who has worked himself up to wealth from small beginnings without external aid, you find ten Scotchmen.' Individual Scots were true globetrotters, seeking out opportunities wherever they arose, from administering Empire in the Indian Civil Service to making bagpipes in Pakistan, from ranching in Argentina to pioneering shipbuilding in Japan. These individuals were, however, less likely to gain immortality than the village postmaster or local inn-keeper who happened to be in the right place at the right time when names were being decided. Robert Balcarres Crawford organised local mail services around the future Abernethy in Saskatchewan. More unusually, he did not name the rural township after himself but after Abernethy Street in Glasgow, where he had been brought up. He did, however, call nearby Balcarres after his middle name.

Being first, however, did not always mean being the winner. Although, for example, Scotsman John Stevenson, who emigrated in 1878, was the first European settler in the future Michigan township of Raber, it honoured Mueller M. Raber, a local lumber pioneer whose company owned the village store, in its adopted name.

Place names are fluid and change over time as settlements evolve and seek a more formal recognition of their status. Names that started out as casual descriptions, such as Ellis Ferry in Ohio or Pile of Bones, Saskatchewan, may end up paying homage to royalty or a colonial governor, sometimes to fulfil the ambition of being recognised as a town or city. The former mining town of Orkney, Kentucky, was once known as the Mouth of Spewing Camp.

Place names are changing again in the post-colonial era, as many countries choose to go back to their aboriginal roots. The redrawing of local government boundaries is another reason for new names emerging. When, for example, a new municipality was formed in Bruce County, Ontario in 1999, it ingeniously blended parts of the three previous names for the township – Brant, Greenock and Walkerton – to create Brockton.

Despite the best efforts of local historians, the origin of some place names has simply been lost through the passage of time. Place names create myths about their origins. With a lack of hard evidence, competing theories abound and assumptions are made that because a place has a Scottish-sounding name it must have a connection with the homeland. Sometimes little or nothing is known about the individual who named a settlement other than that he was 'an early farmer'.

The most common surnames associated with Scotland that have been used in place naming include Anderson, Bell, Cameron, Campbell, Crawford, Davidson, Douglas, Duncan, Fraser, Gordon, Graham, Grant, Hamilton, Henderson, Irving, MacDonald, MacGregor, Melville, Murray, Paterson, Sinclair, Scott, Stewart and Wallace. Bearing one of these Scottish surnames in its name, however, is no guarantee of its Scottish roots. The person in whose honour the town was named might have been a distant descendent of a family from Scotland who emigrated to the USA, or, especially in the case of the Macs, have had an Irish rather than a Scottish ancestry. A few 'Mcs' have no associations with Scotland or Ireland. San Miguel in California was briefly misspelled McGill before restoring its correct name to reflect its roots as a Spanish mission station.

The name Bruce illustrates the variety of associations. Bruce, Wisconsin, was established in 1884 by timber merchant A.C. Bruce, but his nationality has not been established. When the settlers of one of the several Bruces in Manitoba met in 1822 to discuss town names, Neil Gray suggested honouring the Scottish patriot Robert the Bruce. Another Manitoba Bruce was created at the suggestion of a pioneer settler, Andrew Smith, whose family had gained the support of Lord Bruce when they were his tenants on Shetland. Bruce Creek, British Columbia, had previously been known as Boulder Creek, Paradise Creek and Slade Creek until the Geographical Board of Canada changed its name in recognition of St Andrews-born Robert Randolph Bruce, owner of the Paradise mine near the town of Invermere, which he also founded. Mount Bruce in Australia was named in honour of Lieutenant John Bruce, of Scottish parentage, who created a volunteer force after regular troops were withdrawn from the penal colony of Western Australia. Bruce Bay, South Westland, New Zealand, was named after the popular coastal paddle steamer PS *Bruce*, built in Glasgow in 1874.

Some individuals had a much better chance than others to make their mark. Explorers were faced with the challenge of devising hundreds of names for uncharted territory. Whereas they often gave names simply relating to landscape features, such as the Black Mountain or Big Falls, they also remembered other individuals in their expedition team or members of their ship's crew. Other explorers were more imaginative, naming mountains and rivers after famous scientists and geologists. Land surveyors and mapmakers also played a part, as did railway personnel faced with the task of establishing new stations and settlements along the ever expanding railway networks across the wide open spaces of North and South America and Australia.

Landscape also held romantic associations for homesick settlers, as names reminded them of what they'd left behind. Sometimes they simply transplanted the name of their own locality across the oceans. The prefixes 'Ben' and 'Glen' gave a Scottish twist to an otherwise prosaic name, and allusions to the works of iconic authors such as Scott and Burns were also popular. Property developers later drew on the romantic associations with Scotland to create an image that would appeal to prospective purchasers.

Today, communities remain proud of their Scottish roots. Greenock, South Australia, boasts of being 'the little Scotland of the Barossa Valley', while Cape Breton Island is 'the Hebrides on the other side of the Atlantic'.

1

'From Greenland's icy mountains'

The Scots have punched well above their weight as explorers. Inhabiting an infertile land at the edge of the wild North Atlantic may have engendered a natural resourcefulness and ability to cope with privation that made them suited for the role. Driven by curiosity and a thirst for knowledge, some Scots investigated new places for the sheer joy of discovery. Others ventured into unknown territory as missionaries, whalers, surveyors, land speculators, scientists and plant hunters.

Explorers enjoyed several advantages in ensuring that their choice of place name lived on long after they were forgotten. They were often the first Europeans to set foot in a locality, their task being to explore, map and survey it. Naming places could be quite an onerous task if every cape, rocky islet and bay was to be recorded. Their choice of name was also more likely to survive, as usually one of their duties was to report discoveries to a sponsoring body, whether government, the military or a learned society. A written record also provided a more robust and lasting rationale as to why an area was so named rather than folk memory or the changing aspirations of communities, who might give their town or village several different names over time. Explorers also tended to honour their own, with younger generations keeping alive the names of their mentors and heroes.

'Where Afric's sunny fountains . . .'

Although it is in the naming of the world's coldest places that Scottish explorers have had the most lasting impact, a global journey naturally starts with the explorer whose name is a household word in Scotland – David Livingstone. He honoured his queen with the Victoria Falls on the border of Zimbabwe and Zambia.

David Livingstone was arguably the most famous British explorer of the nineteenth century. Born in Blantyre outside Glasgow in 1813, he started work in a cotton mill aged ten before studying theology and medicine at Glasgow University. He realised his ambition to become a medical missionary when posted to the edge of the Kalahari Desert in southern Africa in 1841. This was not enough for Livingstone, however: he wanted to penetrate deep into the heart of Africa in his mission to bring Christianity to new peoples and end the slave trade, which he abhorred.

After sighting the Zambezi River in 1851, Livingstone dedicated four years to tracing its route to the coast. The knowledge gained opened up huge tracts of central and southern Africa and indirectly led to the late nineteenth-century imperialist 'Scramble for Africa'. During the expedition of 1852–56, Livingstone became the first European to set eyes on the future Victoria Falls. In early November 1855, he travelled down the Zambezi to see for himself the area that the natives called the 'smoke that thunders'. Approaching by canoe, Livingstone's party observed the columns of spray and heard the thunderous roar of water miles away from the falls:

> After twenty minutes' sail from Kalai we came in sight, for the first time, of the columns of vapour appropriately called 'smoke,' rising at a distance of five or six miles,

exactly as when large tracts of grass are burned in Africa. Five columns now arose . . . the tops of the columns at this distance appeared to mingle with the clouds. They were white below, and higher up became dark, so as to simulate smoke very closely . . . No one can imagine the beauty of the view from anything witnessed in England. It had never been seen before by European eyes; but scenes so lovely must have been gazed upon by angels in their flight.

Livingstone had discovered one of the world's most spectacular waterfalls. It is here that the 1.2-mile-wide Zambezi River plunges down a series of basalt gorges to a drop of more than 300 feet. Livingstone returned to Britain a hero. Today, the Victoria Falls are a national park and a UNESCO World Heritage site.

Livingstone's travels are also celebrated in the city of Livingstone, Zambia, close to the Victoria Falls. The British started to move into the area during the 1890s, among them the first tourists. The original settlement was at Old Drift, north of the Zambezi, but by 1904 the town had moved to higher ground, which was less infested by mosquitoes. It was named Livingstone in the explorer's honour.

The Victoria Falls Bridge opened the following year as part of Cecil Rhodes' unfulfilled dream to open up Africa from the Cape to Cairo. Today, Livingstone benefits from the millions of tourists who come to see one of the seven natural wonders of the world.

Alexander Bay, Northern Cape, South Africa, celebrates a very different character, Sir James Alexander (1803–85), who was the first person to map the area at the mouth of the Orange River. Africa was one episode in the long and distinguished career of the Clackmannanshire-born military man. After graduating from the universities of Glasgow and Edinburgh and from Sandhurst, he served with the East India Company, the light dragoons in Persia and the 16th Lancers in the Balkans. Swapping regiments again for the Black Watch, he served in Portugal and explored the Essequibo area of the future British Guyana in South America. His next assignment was the Cape Frontier War of 1835. While in South Africa, the Royal Geographical Society provided funding for his exploration of the present-day Republic of Namibia. After the discovery of diamonds in the Northern Cape area in 1925, his South African legacy, Alexander Bay, boomed as a service centre for the mines.

After his exploits as an explorer, Canada beckoned and yet another regiment; this was followed by the Crimea War, where he served as lieutenant-colonel in the Siege of Sevastopol in 1855, and service in New Zealand. After inheriting the estate of Westerton, near Bridge of Allan, Alexander finally settled into local life, as a magistrate and deputy lieutenant for Stirlingshire. Today, he is chiefly remembered for the preservation of Cleopatra's Needle and its shipment to London in 1877. He arranged for various objects to be buried at its base, including photographs of the twelve best-looking English women of the day.

'Advance Australia Fair'

By the time that Port Glasgow-born teacher Peter McCormick composed the song that was to become Australia's national anthem, half a century had passed since Scottish explorers had started to make their mark on the country. In both Australia and New Zealand, exploration was usually a direct precursor to settlement. Teams were dispatched to investigate whether the land was suitable for farming or whether resources were available to support a penal colony.

More Scottish than Welsh – New South Wales

Explorer James Cook, the first person to map 'New South Wales', gave no explanation as to why he chose the name. Scots were among the first to explore and settle the new territory, as penal colony administrators and as convicts, and to take advantage of its vast resources, as sheep farmers and gold miners.

William Paterson (1755-1810), a gardener's son from Kinnettles, near Forfar, became an explorer thanks to the patronage of Lady Strathmore, who shared his interest in botany. In the late 1770s, she backed his travels into the interior of Africa, which he published as *Narrative of Four Journeys into the Country of the Hottentots and Caffraria*. He was responsible for bringing back the first giraffe from South Africa to Britain.

Combining exploration with a military career, Paterson served in India before joining the newly formed New South Wales Corps. In 1793, he led an expedition to find a route through the region's Blue Mountains. He failed, but en route discovered the Grose River, naming it after his commanding officer, Major Francis Grose.

Paterson had a penchant for discovering and naming rivers. In 1804, he was ordered to sail to the then named Van Diemen's Land to found a new settlement at Port Dalrymple. While there he identified and named the South Esk and the North Esk after rivers in his native Angus.

Paterson wasn't the first Scot to make the trip to Tasmania. In 1798, during their voyage to demonstrate that Tasmania was indeed an island, explorers George Bass and Matthew Flinders had named a deep bay at the mouth of the Tamar Estuary Port Dalrymple, after Alexander Dalrymple, the eighteenth-century hydrographer and writer, born at Newhailes outside Edinburgh.

Dalrymple's theory of the existence of a great southern continent inspired James Cook's voyage, which ultimately led to the discovery of the eastern coastline of Australia in 1770. Dalrymple was left at home to nurse his disappointment that he had not been chosen to lead the expedition.

In 1804, two years after Flinders and his Edinburgh-born Lieutenant John Murray had climbed and named Arthur's Seat, Victoria, Paterson's ship arrived on the shores of Tasmania.

His ship, the HMS *Buffalo*, was blown ashore in a gale at Port Dalrymple and a settlement was established. Despite local hostility, he explored up river, locating timber forests and good pasture land during his journey. In 1806 he moved his original settlement to a new site, which he named Patersonia. Paterson later renamed the site Launceston in honour of a governor of New South Wales who was born in the Cornish town, although the name Patersonia still survives as a rural hamlet north-west of Launceston.

Captain Patrick Logan (1791–1830) was another Scot with a taste for naming rivers. Born in Coldingham in Berwickshire and opting for a military career, Logan was ordered to Australia with the 57th Regiment in 1825. The following November he was put in charge of the Moreton Bay Penal Settlement in Queensland. Designed to house re-offending criminals, Moreton Bay had one of the harshest regimes of any penal settlement.

Logan took time out to explore his territory. In 1827 he became the first European to investigate the interior of the mountains which form the present border between New South Wales and Queensland. He named them the McPherson Range after his colleague Major Duncan McPherson.

Logan also travelled upstream from the Moreton settlement, claiming that the river ran through the finest tract of land he had seen in this or any other country. Logan called it the Darling River, not knowing that such a name already existed. To avoid confusion and reward Logan's efficiency, Governor Ralph Darling ordered the name of the new river to be changed to the Logan River. While exploring the Mount Beppo region in 1830, Logan was killed by Aboriginals.

In turn, the Logan River gave its name to a modern city. After Moreton Bay closed, squatters quickly moved in and, following Queensland's separation from New South Wales in 1859, the encouragement of immigration was put on a formal footing. The region grew on the back first of cotton, then sugar and dairying. The urban expansion of nearby Brisbane in the 1960s led to the creation of the new Logan Shire local government district, and on 1 January 1989, Logan was officially declared a city.

Many features of northern Queensland, including Mount Dalrymple, over 4,000 feet high, commemorate George Augustus Frederick Elphinstone Dalrymple: he himself named many more. Dashing, adventurous and impatient of red tape, Dalrymple combined the roles of explorer, administrator and politician. Born in 1826, the tenth son of an Aberdeenshire lieutenant-colonel, he emigrated to Sri Lanka to become a coffee planter. His attention then switched to Australia. Attracted by its empty lands and wide skies, in 1859 he published *Proposals for the Establishment of a New Pastoral Settlement in North Australia*. He attracted sufficient backers to allow him to explore the future Kennedy District around the watershed of the Burdekin River. When the Queensland government countermanded the decision to open the new district for settlement, in compensation Dalrymple was made commissioner for Crown lands. He established the frontier town of Bowen on the Queensland coast in 1861, naming it after Queensland's first colonial governor, Sir George Ferguson Bowen.

Having fallen out with his superiors over the amount of time he spent in the field rather than on paperwork, Dalrymple resigned and took up farming. In 1864 he went exploring inland to the Valley of Lagoons, hacking out a dray route to the coast. Although he entered politics as the first member for Kennedy District, his real love was exploration and he continued his journeys until his death.

The Queensland community of Mitchell on the edge of the Darling Downs also recalls a Scottish explorer, Sir Thomas Livingstone Mitchell. From humble origins in Grangemouth, Mitchell rose to become surveyor general of New South Wales.

Military service during the Peninsular Wars gave him experience of map-making and of gathering topographical intelligence, as well as winning him the patronage of fellow Scot, politician and soldier Sir George Murray. In 1828, with Murray's support, Mitchell was despatched to New South Wales.

His first task as surveyor general was to carry out an investigation of the vast interior with a view to improving the road network. He laid out the route of the Great North Road, linking Sydney to the Hunter Valley, which was built by convict labour between 1826 and 1836. The results of his four expeditions in the 1830s and '40s included proof that all west-flowing rivers in New South Wales were tributaries of the Darling. He discovered and mapped the Western District of Victoria and the Grampian Ranges, which he named after his native mountains.

Across the Grampians, Mitchell found some of the richest grazing land in the world, which he called 'Australia Felix' – Fortunate Australia. For many years, the road into the Western District was known as the Major's Track.

Settlers from Tasmania and New South Wales were soon driving their flocks along the tracks which Mitchell's heavy wagons had cut in 1836. As settlement spread, the Grampians became a vital source of water for farming, as well as for supporting timber production, gold-mining, quarrying and, from the late nineteenth century, tourism.

Today the area embraces the Grampians National Park. Linked by the Glenelg Highway to Melbourne, the township of Dunkeld, Victoria, nestles at the foot of the Grampians. Initially known as Mount Sturgeon, after the 1,070-foot-high peak which Mitchell had named along with Mount Abrupt, early Scottish settlers renamed it Dunkeld.

Mitchell's fourth expedition of 1845–46 took him north from Sydney into what is now Queensland. His aim was to search for an overland route from New South Wales to the north coast along the 'great river' that he was convinced flowed north. His expedition enjoyed mixed success. He failed to find a practicable route to the north coast, or his 'great river', but he did chart an extensive area of unknown country and established that the land to the west of the Darling Downs was suitable for grazing. He was the first European to discover and name the Balonne, Culgoa, Barcoo and Belyando rivers.

Within a few years of Mitchell's report on the area's pastoral potential, squatters had occupied several runs. The main sheep station for Mitchell Downs was located on the site of the present town of Mitchell on the banks of the Maranoa River. After being damaged by floods in 1864, the remains of the sheep station were converted into the Maranoa Hotel, the township's first build-ing. By the mid-1870s Mitchell was an important crossroads and regional centre for south-west Queensland, a position cemented by the opening of a railway station in 1885.

The founding of Mackay, Queensland, is a typical story of 'find your land and farm it', albeit one with a sad ending. Born in Inverness in 1839, John Mackay emigrated to Melbourne with his family in 1854 to join the gold rush. The following year they moved to New South Wales, where his father took up Ness Farm, a sheep run between Uralla and Armidale. George James Macdonald, the local Commissioner for Crown Lands in the late 1830s, turned out to be a better surveyor than speller. He had meant to call the future city after Armadale on Skye, the ancestral seat of his clan.

After turning his hand to gold panning in 1859, Mackay was persuaded by friends to lead an expedition in search of graz-ing land. The party, which included an Irishman, an Italian and an Aboriginal, travelled inland from Armidale, entering terra incognito – the future Mackay district – five months later. Mackay explored the mouth of the river that he found and named it the Mackay River after his father George. Two years later, however, Commodore Burnett of HMS *Pioneer* observed that a Mackay River (now the Tully River) already existed further north and renamed the river and valley Pioneer after his ship. Angered by the name change, Mackay petitioned the governor, who ordered the renaming of the nascent township Mackay in honour of George and John. The tiny settlement prospered on the back of sugar-refining, coal-mining and more recently tourism to become today's city of 85,000 people.

Mackay then established the cattle run called Greenmount in partnership with James Starr, a New England squatter. It was a short and ill-starred venture, as his partner was bankrupt, and Mackay was forced to sell in 1863. He continued his wanderings, discovering a better pass through the Clarke Range than the one that he had used earlier. This gained him nothing other than a long dispute with the Queensland government. He switched from land to sea, sailing the South Pacific under several flags for 18 years, before ending his career as harbourmaster at Brisbane, where he died in 1914.

Two men, two continents

While, for many, exploration was a natural prequel to finding fertile land or opening up communications, some pioneers were also motivated by scientific discovery. One such pioneer was plant hunter James Drummond, who is honoured in Mount Drummond, Western Australia.

Born in Inverarity, Angus, in the winter of 1786, James Drummond grew up with plants, his father being a gardener on the Fotheringham Estate. After becoming curator at Cork Botanical Gardens from 1808, Drummond emigrated with his wife and six children to Australia in 1829. He was appointed to the unpaid position of the Western Australia government's naturalist, earning a small salary as superintendent of the government gardens. During several expeditions across Western Australia, he collected 3,500 specimens of seeds and plants for export to Britain. He also discovered that some local plants were poisonous to livestock, thus solving the mystery of large stock losses in the past.

Drummond often travelled with his family and other botanists. In 1845, his son Johnston was killed by an Aboriginal during an expedition at Moore River. Drummond was so grief-stricken that he abandoned plant collecting for 15 months.

Accompanied by his sons James and John, Drummond gathered together his sixth collection of 225 plants in 1850–51 during a hazardous journey to the Champion Bay district, where the party explored the Murchison River for pastureland. The sons later introduced the first flocks into the region. With his two white packhorses and kangaroo dogs, Drummond Senior became a kent figure throughout the colony. Described as a plain but agreeable old man, his dour Scottish face was framed by bushy white whiskers. He usually walked everywhere, his horses being laden with stores on the way out and specimens on the way home. Once his knapsack and pockets were full, he crammed plants into his hat.

After his retirement in 1855, he held open house on Saturday evenings, entertaining his guests with lectures on natural history. Drummond's legacy was 119 plant species named after him, as well as those which he had personally named. During his exploration of the south coast, Surveyor General John Roe found Drummond's tracks and named Mount Drummond after him.

Not many brothers can claim to have mountains and indeed plants called after them in different continents; however, while James was opening up Western Australia, his brother Thomas was exploring North America. His legacy is Mount Drummond, Alberta.

Thomas Drummond started work at the Elysian Botanic Garden, Doohillock near Forfar, in 1814. During his spell there, he published a book on Scottish mosses. As a result, William Hooker, Professor of Botany at Glasgow University, recommended Thomas as assistant naturalist on Sir John Franklin's second Arctic expedition of 1825-27. While Franklin mapped the Arctic Ocean coast, Thomas explored the Canadian Rockies, discovering more than 500 species of plants. He found the bears very ferocious, driving off their attacks by rattling his specimen box. Wolverines were also a nuisance, stealing drying specimens. While making his 200-mile return journey on snowshoes, Drummond happened to meet an old acquaintance and fellow Scot, David Douglas, of Douglas fir fame.

Returning from Canada, Drummond became the first curator of Belfast Botanic Gardens but still yearned for adventure. In 1831, he sailed for the USA, hoping to join fur traders on their trek north. Illness, however, confined his plant collecting to the area around New Orleans and Texas, where many of the 750 species of plants that he discovered bear his name. He set sail for Havana in Cuba, where he died shortly after landing in 1835.

In 1884, Canadian scientist and explorer George Dawson named the 10,328-foot-high peak in the Rockies and the nearby Drummond Glacier.

Not many explorers have mountains at opposite ends of the globe named by or for them. Sir James Hector was one such adventurer. Shortly after graduating, the Edinburgh-born and trained doctor was appointed geologist and botanist on the Palliser expedition of 1857-60. He was recommended by fellow Scot Sir Roderick Murchison, Director General of the British Geological Survey. The expedition had two goals – to prospect routes for the Canadian Pacific Railway and to collect new plant species. Hector named the 11,476-foot-high Mount Lyell, which straddles the boundary between Alberta and British Columbia, after the early-nineteenth-century Scottish geologist Sir Charles Lyell.

Lyell promoted the work of fellow Scot James Hutton in establishing that the earth was very old and changed very gradually, much to the consternation of religious opinion of the day. Separately, Lyell is commemorated within Yosemite National Park, California, by the Lyell Glacier, Lyell Canyon and Mount Lyell, the park's highest peak.

Hector is also commemorated at the spot where he nearly lost his life, with two icons of the Rockies: Kicking Horse Pass and Kicking Horse River on the border of British Columbia and Alberta. For three years, the Palliser team of five crisscrossed the Prairies, mapping, charting, assembling magnetic and weather records, and gathering detailed botanical, zoological and geological data. To cover the enormous distances, the team sometimes split up to carry out individual missions. In August 1859, Hector set out in search of mountain passes. At his camp near Wapta Falls, a packhorse bolted and Hector gave chase. As he rounded up the horse, it kicked him, breaking his ribs and knocking him unconscious. Assuming that he was dead, his guides began to dig his grave. Hector proved them wrong and continued to follow a river to the summit pass.

Towards the end of his adventurous life, Hector revisited the site of this legendary accident. He recalled, 'When I regained consciousness, my grave was dug and they were preparing to put me in it. So that's how Kicking Horse got its name.' Today, both the Canadian Pacific Railway and the Trans-Canada Highway cross the pass and every tourist is told the story of Hector and the horse.

Again on Murchison's recommendation, in 1862 Hector arrived in Otago, New Zealand, to carry out a geological survey in the hope of finding useful minerals. He undertook this despite the Otago gold rush already being in full swing. Over the next 40 years, he established himself as the premier scientific figure in New Zealand society. Fellow Scot James McKerrow paid tribute to him in the 5,016-foot-high Mount Hector, North Island.

Hector's legacy is remarkable: Hector, a settlement on New Zealand's west coast; Hector Lake in Alberta; the Hector River in New Zealand's North Island; Hector Island in the Canadian Arctic; and 11 new species of wildlife, including Hector's Dolphin.

The snow-clad, jagged peaks of the Canadian Rockies proved not only an almost insurmountable obstacle to communications but also a magnet for explorers. In Alberta, David Douglas named two peaks, Mount Brown and Mount Hooker, as well as having a third, the 10,600-foot-high Mount Douglas, named in his honour.

Douglas was a remarkable man. Born in Scone, Perthshire, in 1798, he left school aged 11 to work as a gardener on a local estate before moving to Glasgow's Botanic Gardens. There he met Robert Brown, the botanist from Montrose who was the first person to observe and name the nucleus of the cell. Douglas also worked with William Hooker, the newly appointed Professor of Botany at the university. Hooker asked Douglas to lead a plant-hunting expedition to North America on behalf of the Horticultural Society of London.

Douglas's first expedition to the relatively settled eastern regions in search of new fruit and vegetables was such a success that he was recruited to undertake a more ambitious venture to explore the north-west seaboard. After an eight-month voyage round Cape Horn and an investigation of the region round

Vancouver, he travelled over 7,000 miles inland. His ascent of Mount Brown in 1827 was only the second peak in the Rockies to be climbed by a European. He wrote of his crossing of the Athabasca Pass:

> Nothing can be seen, in every direction as far as the eye can reach, except mountains towering above each other, rugged beyond description. This peak, the highest yet known in the northern continent of America, I feel a sincere pleasure in naming 'Mount Brown'. . . . A little to the southward is one nearly the same height, rising into a sharper point. This I named 'Mount Hooker'.

For many years, geographers and mountaineers were puzzled by Douglas's two giants. It turned out that he had overestimated the altitude of the Athabasca Pass by nearly 6,000 feet. The late nineteenth-century mountaineer Norman Collie finally solved the mystery by a careful reading of Douglas's journals. It was simply not possible that Douglas could have climbed such a peak in an afternoon when snow lay thickly on the ground. Mounts Forbes, Columbia, Bryce and Alberta supplanted Mounts Brown and Hooker as the highest peaks in the Canadian Rockies. Mapmaker George Dawson named Mount Douglas in 1884 in the plant hunter's honour. The peak is sometimes referred to as the Black Douglas because it is less often snow-capped than its neighbour, the White Douglas, reflecting the ancestral names of two branches of the Scottish family. The official name of the latter is Mount St Bride, after the saint associated with the church where Douglas chiefs were buried. Another peak in the Rockies is named Mount Sir Douglas in honour of the First World War commander, Sir Douglas Haig, rather than the explorer.

On this trip, Douglas sent back the seeds of more than 800 species, 130 of which flourished well in Britain, the two areas sharing a temperate, maritime climate. Among these were the Douglas fir, the Sitka spruce, the Noble fir, the Grand fir and the Radiata, or Monterey pine. In total, 200 plants are called after Douglas, the greatest number ever associated with one person.

Returning to Britain in 1827, Douglas could not settle. Two years later he was back on his travels, this time further south to the region around the Columbia River. After about a thousand miles, he aborted his attempt to reach Alaska, believing it to be too ambitious, and decided instead to return to Vancouver by canoe down the Fraser River. Unfortunately, he lost his seed collection and instruments when his fragile craft capsized. Douglas then moved much further south. While exploring Hawaii in 1833, he was gored to death in a pit trap dug for wild cattle into which a bull had already fallen. Whether Douglas fell as a result of his damaged eyesight or was the victim of foul play was never proven.

The hunt for fur

For centuries, the Rocky Mountains proved a natural barrier to opening up much of the vast interior of Canada. The demand for beaver pelts, whose softness and resilience made an excellent material when felted for men's hats, provided the impetus to drive exploration north and west in search of trade routes in the nineteenth century. Thanks to over-hunting, beaver populations in the east had dwindled dramatically. The desperate search for new sources of beaver pelts led to increasingly bloody competition between the two major trading companies, the Hudson's Bay Company (HBC) and the North West Company (NWC). The search for new routes turned traders into explorers. Two Scottish NWC employees played a very significant role in mapping Canada west of the Rockies and in discovering the rivers that bear their names.

The Mackenzie River, Northwest Territories, Canada's largest river system, owes its name to one of Scotland's most remarkable explorers, Sir Alexander Mackenzie. He was the first European to reach both the Arctic and the Pacific overland. Although his motive was trade, it is as an explorer that he is remembered today. Born on the Hebridean island of Lewis, Mackenzie emigrated with his father and two aunts to join his uncle in New York in 1774. Being from a loyalist family during the American Wars of Independence, young Mackenzie was despatched to safety and school in Montreal. Adventure soon beckoned in the shape of the fur trade. After five office-bound years in Montreal, Mackenzie tried his hand at trading. He impressed his employer sufficiently to offer him a share in the business provided that he accepted a posting in the increasingly competitive far west.

After postings to the Churchill River area of Saskatchewan and Athabasca, Alberta, in 1789, Mackenzie prepared to descend the 'Grand River', which would later bear his name. He described its exploration as 'this favourite project of my own ambition'. His party, which included a Chipewyan Indian accompanied by his wives and retainers, made good progress. They descended the 1,080-mile-long river in a fortnight by canoe, averaging 75 miles a day. The ocean at the mouth, however, turned out to be the Arctic rather than the Pacific, thanks to errors in existing maps. Mackenzie called his discovery the River of Disappointment, but it soon took his name.

Mackenzie already had a second expedition in mind in his quest to find a route to the Pacific. He followed the advice of an experienced local guide that over the mountains beyond the headwaters of the Peace River he would find a river flowing west. He turned out to be more reliable than any map. After many vicissitudes, and averaging a remarkable 20 miles a day, his party finally reached the Pacific near Bella Coola, where he inscribed on a rock, 'Alexander Mackenzie from Canada by land, 22 July 1793'. This expedition made Mackenzie the first person to cross the American continent north of Mexico. His leadership ensured that his party returned from the 2,300-mile journey to the Pacific and back safe and well, although the strain provoked what amounted to a breakdown. Mackenzie left the west, spending several years back in Montreal, reorganising the NWC, before writing up his journeys and briefly entering politics. By 1812, he decided to retire to Scotland and marry 14-year-old Geddes Mackenzie, who was more than 30 years his junior. He spent his final years largely on the estate of Avoch in Easter Ross, which Geddes and her twin sister had inherited.

Although Mackenzie had added a huge tract to the map of Canada, his exploration turned out to be of no immediate use to his employer. Only after his death were many of his ideas for a continent-wide fur trade adopted. As well as the Mackenzie River, other areas of Canada bearing the explorer's name include Mackenzie Bay and Mackenzie Island. The Mackenzie Mountains, however, while also in the wilderness of the Yukon through which the Mackenzie River flows, are not named after the explorer but after Alexander Mackenzie, Canada's second prime minister, who was born in Logierait in Perthshire.

A postscript to the story involves both Mackenzies. When travelling up the Mackenzie River in 1937, the author and Governor-General of Canada John Buchan learned of the rugged, almost inaccessible region of the South Nahanni River, flowing from the Mackenzie Mountains. The stories of mine prospectors who had gone into the region never to be heard of again added to the mystique. He noted that the 'South Nahanni fascinates me, and I want to make a trip there . . . before I leave

Canada', a wish that was not realised. He had to rely on his imagination to create the wilderness setting for his novel, *Sick Heart River*, published posthumously in 1941.

The Fraser River, British Columbia, is named after the eponymous NWC employee who shared Mackenzie's ambition to find a fur-trade route to the Pacific. Simon Fraser pioneered the permanent settlement of the area now known as British Columbia and was the first European to trace the future Fraser River from source to mouth, including Fraser Canyon upstream from the delta on which Vancouver now stands.

Fraser's parents were Roman Catholics who, like many other Highlanders of their faith, emigrated to New York in 1773 to practise their religion freely. They settled on a farm in Vermont, where Fraser was born. After the father was killed fighting on the loyalist side during the American Wars of Independence, the family moved to a brother's farm west of Montreal. Apprenticed to the NWC in 1792, little is known of Fraser's early career, although it was clearly successful. He was appointed a partner aged only 25.

In 1805, Fraser was charged with extending NWC's operations west of the Rockies. The plan was to descend the river whose exploration Alexander Mackenzie had abandoned after hearing reports from First Nation people of impassable rapids and canyons. Fraser was accompanied by John Stuart from Nethybridge in Inverness-shire and James McDougall, born in Montreal of Highland parentage. Fraser and McDougall established Trout Lake Fort (later Fort McLeod), the first permanent white settlement west of the Canadian Rockies. Stuart established a second post at what he called the Carriers' Lake, now named Stuart Lake after him.

Before setting off on his 1806 exploration, Fraser sent the winter's harvest of furs to the trading post at Dunvegan on the Peace River. It included 14 packs from Trout Lake – the first furs traded west of the Rockies. It was May before the ice allowed Fraser and Stuart to start their journey. They encountered many difficulties, from unskilled canoe men to rapids, rocks and fallen trees. Lack of provisions finally forced Fraser to postpone his mission and instead he built the future Fort Fraser trading post beside the future Lake Fraser. He named the area New Caledonia because, it is believed, the country reminded him of his mother's descriptions of the Scottish Highlands. Exploration had to be delayed for a further year as supplies and men did not arrive until the autumn of 1807. Fraser passed the time by establishing the Fort George trading post. At the end of May 1808, the party of 24, including two First Nation guides, finally set out. Fraser soon had to abandon travel by water because the river was in spate, although travel on land proved almost equally hazardous. He wrote, 'We had to pass where no human being should venture.'

Fraser adopted a friendly approach to the First Nation people whose territories they passed through. All went well until he reached the mouth of the river, where the Cowichans proved hostile. He was chased back upstream by scores of canoes. He had difficulty in stopping some of his men deserting and finding their own way back to Fort George. He finally reached the coast on 6 August. The journey down the river had taken 36 days and the return trip added another 37. Although the expedition iden-tified the exact source of the river which rises in the Rockies' Fraser Pass, Fraser felt that the expedition had failed. The river was no use as a transport route: Fraser, like Mackenzie before him, had hoped that the river that became the Fraser was in fact the Columbia River, whose lower reaches had been observed by several explorers and traders. Four years after Fraser's journey, fellow NWC employee David Thompson became the first per-son to travel the length of the Columbia.

Fraser continued to work for the NWC. For much of the time, he was in charge of its Mackenzie River District, but he was unhappy with the violence of the clashes between NWC and HBC employees, which culminated in the Red River massacre of 1816. Fraser was arrested and tried with five other partners for treason. After his acquittal, he settled to a life as a farmer on the Raisin River, near St Andrews, Ontario. He died on 18 August 1862, his wife dying the next day. The journey down the Fraser was re-enacted in 1958, the 150th anniversary, as part of British Columbia's centenary celebrations.

An employee of the rival Hudson's Bay Company pushed the frontiers of its influence even further north. Robert Campbell was the first European to penetrate the Yukon Territory. Modestly, he did not name any landscape features after himself, but his legacy, named by others in his honour, includes Mount Campbell and the Robert Campbell Highway built in 1968.

After assisting his father on his sheep farm in Glen Lyon, Perthshire, Campbell emigrated in 1830 to work for the HBC. He was initially employed to introduce sheep from Kentucky to the Red River Settlement, but when the experiment failed, he requested a transfer to the HBC's fur-trading arm and was assigned to the Mackenzie River District. As a result of speculation that the area to the west was rich in furs, Campbell was directed to explore the northern branches of the Liard River system. In 1840, he pushed up to Frances Lake in the Yukon, which he named in honour of Frances Ramsay Simpson, wife of the Dingwall-born governor of the HBC. Continuing overland, he became the first white man to cross into the Yukon River watershed from the east.

In 1843, Campbell set off on his travels again, descending the Pelly River to its confluence with another substantial river, which he called the Lewes and which is now known as the Yukon River, where a new HBC trading post, Fort Selkirk, briefly opened in 1848. Either failing to realise that most features already had First Nation people names or finding them hard to pronounce, Campbell named the Pelly River after Sir John Pelly, an HBC governor, and Fort Selkirk, after Thomas Douglas, 5th Earl of Selkirk, the founder of the Red River Settlement.

Members of the hostile Chilkat tribe raided Fort Selkirk, forcing Campbell into a boat, which they set adrift. According to oral tradition, the Fort Selkirk First Nation chief, Hanan, rescued him and a grateful Campbell gave Hanan his name. Hanan's son, Big Jonathan Campbell, was chief of the Selkirk First Nation from 1916–58. After the raid, no white man came near Fort Selkirk for nearly 40 years. Although Campbell was keen to try and find a way to the Pacific, he was directed to explore the route between Fort Selkirk and Fort Yukon, completing his final expedition to the north in 1851.

Finding Sir John Franklin

The Northwest Passage, linking the Atlantic and the Pacific, was the Holy Grail that took explorers to the wastes of northern Canada. The potential route through the Arctic Ocean and the archipelago of islands off Canada would open up trade from Europe to the Far East. From King Henry VII's dispatching of John Cabot in 1497 to find a route to the Orient, expedition after expedition had set out and failed. It was not until 1906 that Roald Amundsen finally navigated the Passage before becoming the first person to reach the South Pole.

Amundsen put the last piece of the puzzle of the Northwest Passage into place by sailing through the Simpson Strait, which runs between King William Island and the Canadian mainland. It was named after Thomas Simpson, born in Dingwall in 1805.

His cousin George, governor of the HBC, employed Simpson as his secretary on his graduation from King's College, Aberdeen. Over the winter of 1836–37 Simpson snowshoed from Fort Garry to Fort Chipewyan on Lake Athabasca, a staggering 1,277 miles in 46 days.

Simpson then joined the HBC-commissioned expedition of 1837–39 under Peter Warren Dease to complete the survey of the Arctic. He explored the coastline west of the Mackenzie River, journeyed down the Coppermine River, and in December 1839, after discovering the Simpson Strait and naming Victoria Island, set out for Red River from the Boothia Peninsula. This time he covered 1,800 miles in 61 days. Having reached Barrow Point in the Canadian Arctic, he was close to exploring and charting the Northwest Passage.

Ordered by his cousin to return to England, Simpson set off overland to New York by horse. According to his companions, he became increasingly anxious and even deranged during the journey, which ended with two of the party dead from gunshot wounds and Simpson with his head blown off. The local investigating justice regarded it as a case of murder and suicide, the latter being a crime in the eyes of Victorian society. Simpson was buried in an unmarked grave. He was thus deprived of the knowledge that his cousin's order had been over-ruled and he was free to continue his exploration; he had also been given the honour of the gold medal of the Royal Geographical Society. Only Simpson's brother Alexander sprang to his defence, publishing the theory that Thomas fired in self-protection when he realised that his companions were planning to steal and sell his notes and maps to an American rival. In his view, they then murdered Thomas in retaliation.

In 1845, Sir John Franklin led one of many expeditions to find the Northwest Passage. When news of its fate and that of the

129 men on board its two ships failed to reach Britain, Sir John's wife led a campaign to pressurise the Admiralty to send out a search party. The person who led the first party in the *Lady Franklin* was whaling captain William Penny, after whom the vast Penny Ice Cap on Baffin Island is named. He is also remembered in the Penny Strait, Nunavut, which runs between Bathurst Island and Devon Island in the Canadian Arctic, and the Penny Highlands on Baffin Island, whose ancient granite peaks rise to over 6,900 feet.

Born in Peterhead in 1809, Penny followed his father into the whaling trade at the age of 12. For more than four decades, he sailed almost every year to the Arctic whaling and sealing grounds. In 1839, he entered unexplored waters off Baffin Island, searching for a large whaling ground in an inlet known to the indigenous people as 'Tenudiakbeek'. Failing to find it, he returned to Scotland with a guide named Eenoolooapik, who accompanied him the next year on the British Whaling and Exploring expedition. This time they found Tenudiakbeek, which Penny called Hogarth's Sound after the owner of his ship, *Neptune*. Although large numbers of whales migrated into the Sound in early September, Penny returned to Scotland empty-handed, having failed to capture one.

After fruitless searches of Lancaster Sound in 1847 and 1849 for a sighting of Franklin's ships, Penny won Admiralty backing to lead an expedition in 1850. His party found Franklin's 1845–46 winter quarters on Beechey Island, explored Wellington Sound, where he found bits of debris, discovered Queens Channel and sighted the strait that now bears his name. Penny eventually dropped out of the Franklin search, frustrated by the overbearing attitude of the Admiralty and by the public reaction that his expeditions had not achieved enough.

Penny redirected his energies back to whaling and the establishment of a Christian mission on Baffin Island, reflecting his concerns that whaling had introduced disease and an alien culture to the native people. He was among the early promoters of steam whalers, taking command of one of the new Dundee steamers, *Polynia*, on her maiden voyage in 1861. Two years later he retired from the sea to Aberdeen, where he died in 1892.

Orcadian John Rae was the man who finally solved the Victorian cause célèbre, the mystery surrounding the fate of Sir John Franklin and his men. One of Scotland's greatest explorers, Rae was modest in life and in the place names left behind him. Even the tiny community of Rae/Edzo, on Great Slave Lake, Northwest Territories, has reverted to its Inuit name, Behchoko. Rae would have approved of the name change, as one of his strengths as an explorer was learning to speak local dialects. On graduating as a doctor from Edinburgh University, like so many Orcadians before and after him Rae joined the HBC, his father being the company's Stromness agent. He served for ten years as surgeon at Moose Factory, the company's trading post on James Bay. Here, he spent his leisure hours learning the skills essential to survival in the Arctic – hunting, fishing, sledge-hauling, snowshoe walking and camping.

After being chosen by the HBC to complete its survey of the northern coastline of North America, Rae set out in 1846 with ten men and an Inuit interpreter and his son in two small boats. Deterred by ice and storms, the party had to winter on Repulse Bay, where they built Fort Hope and adopted local ways, eating fish and game and sleeping in igloos. The next spring Rae and his men managed to link up their survey with that of John and James Clark. On his return Rae learned of his promotion to chief trader.

Rae had joined the search for Sir John Franklin in 1848. The party made a possibly record-breaking trip by canoe from around Toronto to the mouth of the Mackenzie River in 96 days. Rae

explored the Rae River, later named after him, before returning without success. At the Admiralty's request he resumed his
search for Franklin in 1851. Unfortunately, pack ice prevented
him from reaching King William Island, where the Franklin
expedition was believed to have met its tragic end. However,
Rae did manage to bring back two pieces of wood from one of
Sir John's ill-fated ships, *Erebus* or *Terror*.

In 1853, Rae set off to complete his mapping of the north
coast. He discovered the entrance to an unknown, 200-mile-
long river off Chesterfield Inlet, which he named the Quoich.
Despite some authorities assuming that Quoich was an Inuit
word, he appears to have named it after a glen and river in
Inverness-shire, although what the landscape's resonance for
Rae was is not recorded. Maybe he simply liked the sound of
the word. Rae's discovery that King William Land was, in fact,
an island separated from the Boothia Peninsula was of sufficient
importance that the stretch of water was later named the Rae
Strait. He is also commemorated in the Rae Isthmus, separating
the Melville Peninsula from mainland Canada.

The next spring the Inuit provided him with the first con-
crete evidence of the location of Franklin's party – silver cutlery,
a cap band and tales of more than 30 men who had starved to
death. Rae's ability to speak the local dialect allowed the details
of what had happened to emerge. The Inuits had seen a party
of white men dragging sledges down the west coast of King
William Island. They were thin and hungry and some fell down
as they walked. The Inuits had later found up to 40 bodies on
the seashore: some were buried, some were in tents and a few
were huddled under a boat. The Inuits' description of the terrain
allowed Rae to pinpoint the exact spot.

On arrival in London in 1854, Rae reported his findings about
the fate of Franklin, including the view that the last survivors

may have resorted to cannibalism. The report caused a sensation. Rae was criticised for not verifying the Inuits' reports personally, for accepting the story of 'savages' and for rushing home to claim the £10,000 reward offered by Lady Franklin. This was Rae's only reward: unlike the other main players in the Franklin saga, he never received a knighthood. His exploration of the Arctic was effectively at an end.

One Scot had the distinction of both serving on two of Franklin's expeditions and working with John Rae in the search to discover his fate, the explorer, surgeon and natural historian Sir John Richardson. The Richardson River, Nunavut, in the Canadian Arctic is one of several natural features named after him.

Born in Dumfries into a prosperous brewing family in 1787, Richardson was one of twelve children. Poet and Dumfries exciseman Robert Burns was a close family friend who influenced the young man's literary tastes. After training as a doctor, Richardson volunteered for the navy, where he saw action in the Napoleonic Wars and the American War of 1812. Returning to Edinburgh to complete his medical studies, he practised as a doctor in Leith before serving as surgeon and naturalist on Franklin's first expedition of 1819–22 to map the north coast of Canada. It is thanks to Richardson's ministrations that the loss of life from cold and starvation was not higher: Franklin had earned the nickname of 'the man who ate his boots' because hunger reduced his men to chewing lichen and leather.

Undeterred, Richardson signed on as second-in-command on Franklin's second Arctic expedition in 1824. This included exploring the coast east of the mouth of the Mackenzie River and a canoe survey of the shores of the Great Slave Lake. Thereafter Richardson spent a decade in England as chief medical officer at the Melville Hospital, Chatham. After his first wife's death, he married a niece of Sir John Franklin and spent much of his spare time writing the authoritative scientific works that established him as one of the foremost biologists of his era. In 1838, he was promoted as senior physician at the Royal Naval Hospital, Haslar, at the time the largest naval hospital in the world and the biggest brick building in Europe. Richardson made his final trip to the Arctic in 1848 on a sadder mission, to look for his erstwhile leader, whom only his responsibilities at Haslar had prevented him from joining. He returned the next year, leaving John Rae in command of the expedition, which was a model of organisation and care for the crew.

Sir George Nares gave his name to several features, including the Nares Strait and Nares Land in Greenland, Nares Harbour in the Admiralty Islands, the Nares Deep in the North Atlantic, two Nares Capes in the Canadian Arctic, and Mount Nares, Victoria Land, in Antarctica. Nares was an accidental Scot. He was born on 24 April 1831, probably at Straloch House, Newmachar in Aberdeenshire, where his family were staying. By the time of his baptism at Llansanffraid, he had returned home to Wales. After his mother's death, however, his father married Susan Ramsay, the widow of the owner of Straloch, where Nares spent much of his childhood.

Nares entered the Royal Navy in 1845, cutting his naval and polar teeth on the search for Franklin. His oceanographical research when captain of the *Shearwater* in the early 1870s led to his appointment as captain of HMS *Challenger*, dispatched by the government in December 1872 on a three-year circumnavigation devoted to exploring the deep oceans. Nares commanded the expedition for the first two years until, satisfied by the smooth running of the project, the government recalled him to lead the British Arctic expedition of 1875–76, the chief aim of which was to reach the North Pole. Nares travelled further north than any previous expedition, but he aborted the voyage when some of the crew developed scurvy. His last expedition was at the other end of the globe: a survey of the stormy Strait of Magellan between the Atlantic and the Pacific.

Pole to Pole

Nares was not alone in being associated with both Sir John Franklin and the globe's iciest regions. Sir John Ross and his nephew, Sir James Clark Ross, account for a remarkable number of the world's coldest place names, from Boothia in the Arctic to the Ross Sea in Antarctica.

A son of the manse, John Ross was born in 1777 in Inch near Stranraer. After spells with the merchant navy and with the East India Company, he served in the Royal Navy during the Napoleonic Wars as midshipman, lieutenant and commander.

Only after peace was declared did the centuries-old search for the Northwest Passage through the Davis Strait resume. In 1818, Ross was appointed to the *Isabella*, a hired whaler, as joint commander with Lieutenant William Edward Parry of the *Alexander*. Young James Clark Ross sailed with his uncle. When Ross tried to proceed west through Lancaster Sound, he was deceived by a mirage, describing his passage as being barred by what he thought was a range of mountains. He named the capes on either side of Smith Sound after his ships, the Alexander and the Isabella. On his return, Ross was promoted and wrote an account of his voyage. Then things turned sour, as his critics started to doubt the reality of what he had named the Croker Mountains. Not many Secretaries to the Admiralty have had the honour of having a mirage called after them. Parry was sent to investigate and returned with proof of the range's non-existence. Even Ross's nephew James turned against him.

Ross had to cool his heels until 1829, when he was offered another opportunity to look for the Northwest Passage, joining an expedition largely funded by Felix Booth, the gin magnate. Ross took command of the steam vessel *Victory*, still a novelty at the time, and was joined again by his nephew, James. Frozen seas meant that little progress was made and Ross was forced to abandon his ship in 1832 when it became stuck fast in the ice. Ross and his men made their way to Fury Beach, where they wintered in a hut made out of the wreck of the HMS *Fury*, abandoned with its stores by a previous Arctic expedition under William Parry, before eventually returning to Britain. All was not lost. The expedition surveyed and named the Boothia Peninsula and the Gulf of Boothia, acknowledging the expedition's sponsor, and King William Land, honouring the elderly monarch William IV. Young James discovered the North Magnetic Pole during a sledge journey on the Boothia Peninsula.

This time Ross was feted on his return, being knighted in 1834 and heaped with honours by scientific and learned societies. Again, he published a book of his travels and again he fell out with his nephew, and later with his Polar colleagues. It was only in 1849, largely financed by himself, Sir Felix Booth and by public subscription, that Ross was able to set out from Stranraer on another Arctic expedition. This time it was to search for Sir John Franklin. With the support of the official naval search party, he discovered three graves and other evidence that Franklin had wintered in Lancaster Sound. Further searches proved futile and Ross returned home for the last time to continue his quarrels with polar authorities until his death in 1876.

Sir James Clark Ross picked up the icy torch, serving both with his uncle and with explorer William Parry. In 1827, he was second in command on the Hecla expedition during which Parry tried to reach the North Pole over the ice and created the

The Antarctic Scots

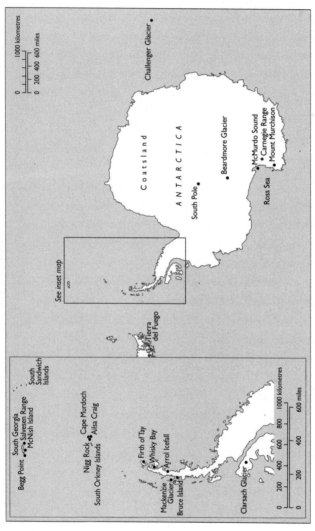

Scots are among those who have been honoured in place names within the vast icy desert of Antarctica and its offshore islands. Those represented on the map are only a small selection – many others also exist. Faced with a blank, white canvas, explorers James Clark Ross and William Speirs Bruce of the Scotia expedition (Scottish National Antarctic expedition of 1902–04) were prolific in naming landscape features, and whalers also made their mark. Place names include references to explorers' nearest and dearest, crew members and sponsors, along with acknowledged Scottish experts in the fields of geology, medicine and physics.

Ailsa Craig: Named by William Speirs Bruce of the Scotia expedition because its shape reminded him of the island in the Firth of Clyde.

Arrol Icefall: Named by the UK Antarctic Place-names Committee after the Arrol-Johnston car, which was adapted for use by Shackleton's Antarctic expedition of 1907–09. It was the first mechanical transport used in Antarctica.

Begg Point: Named after Captain Sinclair Begg, a Caithness-born employee of the Leith whaling company, Christian Salvesen. He managed the South Georgia Whaling Co. station at Leith Harbour from 1947 to 1951.

Bruce Island: Chosen by Scottish geologist David Ferguson, who made a geological reconnaissance from the whale catcher *Hanka* in 1913 to honour William Speirs Bruce. Ferguson also named Inverleith Hill.

Cape Murdoch: Named by William Speirs Bruce after a supporter, the Scottish painter W.G. Burn Murdoch, artist on the *Balaena*, one of the Dundee whaling ships in the Antarctic in 1892–93.

Carnegie Range: One of the more unusual locations at which the Dunfermline-born US industrialist and philanthropist is celebrated.

Challenger Glacier: Commemorating the work of the Challenger expedition of 1872–76, which explored ocean depths, headquartered in Edinburgh.

Clarsach Glacier: So-called because its shape resembles the Scottish harp.

Firth of Tay: Named, along with Cape Scrymgeour, by Captain Thomas Robertson on a Dundee whaling expedition of 1892–93.

Mackenzie Glacier: Chosen by the UK Antarctic Place-names Committee for Sir James Mackenzie, the pioneering cardiologist born in Scone in 1853.

McNish Island: Named after the rebellious Glaswegian carpenter Harry 'Chippy' McNish, who joined Shackleton on his dash to South Georgia to seek help in 1916.

Mount Murchison: Named by James Clark Ross after the famous Scottish geologist Roderick Impey Murchison.

Nigg Rock: Charted and named by William Speirs Bruce after the birthplace of his wife in Ross and Cromarty. He gave the Mackenzie Peninsula her maiden name.

Salvesen Range: Acknowledging Sir Harold Salvesen of the Leith whaling company, who supported the South Georgia Survey of 1951–54.

Whisky Bay: Associated with nearby Brandy Bay, where a member of an Antarctic expedition suggested brandy as a cure for a dog bite.

record of 82° 45' N, one which stood unchallenged until 1875. It was, however, still 500 miles south of the Pole. Parry named Cape James Ross on Melville Island in the Arctic after him.

From 1839 to 1843, Ross switched his attention to the Antarctic, tasked by the Admiralty to find the South Magnetic Pole. The expedition's ships, *Erebus* and *Terror*, anchored in a natural harbour on New Zealand's sub-Antarctic Auckland islands while a shore party investigated the potential of setting up a sealing station before heading south. The harbour was later renamed Port Ross.

Penetrating the pack ice, Ross discovered the Ross Sea, Ross Island and the Ross Ice Shelf, the immense barrier that impeded his journey further into the interior. Features that he identified and named after others include Victoria Land and the McMurdo Sound. He christened two volcanoes on Ross Island, Mount Erebus and Mount Terror, after his ships. Scots geologist Roderick Murchison and Scots pioneer of optics David Brewster were among the scientists honoured with Mount Murchison and Mount Brewster. As Antarctica had no previous human history, every feature was virgin territory to be named. Like his uncle before him, on his return to Britain, Ross was knighted and feted in learned circles. It is said that he promised his newly wed wife that he would abandon polar research. She released him from his promise to lead the first expedition to search for Sir John Franklin. Ross never fully recovered from her death in 1857.

The largest community on the Antarctic continent today is McMurdo Station on McMurdo Sound, which Ross named after a Dumfriesshire-born lieutenant on the *Terror*.

Peterhead-born Thomas Abernethy was a veteran of polar exploration and a gunner on the *Erebus* during James Ross's Antarctic expedition of 1842. It was not Ross, however, but the UK Antarctic Place-names Committee who chose to name the

Abernethy Flats, a gravel plain on James Ross Island, after him in 1983.

It was to be half a century before anyone other than the occasional whaler or sealer set foot on the continent of ice. Led by William Speirs Bruce, Scotland made its own contribution to polar discovery through the Scottish National Antarctic expedition of 1902-04. This venture also added more names to the 'Scottish' map, from Ailsa Craig in the South Orkney Islands to Coats Land in Antarctica.

Although Bruce was born in London, he returned to his family roots as a medical student at Edinburgh University. His interests in oceanography and marine biology were aroused by a stint in the office of the Challenger expedition and by a course delivered by Professor Patrick Geddes in an old barge which his students called 'The Ark'. Before he could complete his studies, Bruce was offered the chance of a lifetime, as naturalist and surgeon on a Dundee whaling expedition to the Antarctic in 1892. With whales being over-fished in the Arctic, the search for new whaling grounds was becoming urgent. The expedition sailed as far as Ross Island, where Bruce's ship *Balaena* anchored on the ice in Ross's Erebus and Terror Gulf. Although few whales were found, the expedition paid for itself by slaughtering hundreds of seals, an activity which Bruce personally hated.

Bruce's appetite for exploration had been whetted: 'I am burning to be off again anywhere, but particularly to the far south where I believe there is a vast sphere for research.' Failing to raise money for an expedition to South Georgia, Bruce had to be content with serving on the staff of the Ben Nevis Observatory. He did manage trips to the Arctic, as naturalist on the Jackson-Harmsworth expedition of 1896, on the oceanographic research ship *Princess Alice* belonging to the future Prince Albert I of Monaco, and on the yacht of wealthy thread manufacturer Andrew Coats of Paisley.

Andrew Coats and his brother made it financially possible for Bruce to realise his dream of leading an Antarctic expedition: his application to join Scott on the *Discovery* had been accepted too late for him to sail. The Coats family contributed £30,000 towards the £36,405 raised for the venture, the British government having refused funding. Bruce refitted a Norwegian whaler as his ship, renaming her *Scotia*. Captain Robertson from Peterhead, an old hand, with 20 years' experience of Arctic ice, was in charge: all but two of *Scotia*'s 26 crew members were experienced Scottish seafarers. Bruce appointed six scientific staff, including a taxidermist and an artist.

Crowds lined the quayside at Troon to wave *Scotia* off on 2 November 1902. The local press were less happy at this breach of the Sabbath: 'Stands Scotland where she did, when a ship's company can sail on the Sabbath with pipes playing and people singing, not psalms but profane songs such as *Auld Lang Syne*.' After taking on two years' worth of provisions in the Falkland Islands, *Scotia* made it nearly as far south as sealer James Weddell before the pack ice closed in and they sailed north to winter on the South Orkneys at Scotia Bay. Chief engineer Allan George Ramsay died from a heart problem over the winter and was buried at the foot of the 1,560-foot-high peak that Bruce named Mount Ramsay, to the sound of a piper playing 'Flowers of the Forest'.

After calling in at the Falklands and a sojourn in Argentina, Bruce headed south again, sighting land on 3 March 1904. On several occasions it looked as if the pack ice would trap their ship for the winter. On 12 March, Bruce triumphantly wrote in *Scotia*'s log:

Soon after 11a.m. we hoisted our flags . . . Thus for the first time in 81 years, and only for the second time in the history of the South Polar exploration, the Union

Jack flew south of 74°S. I got all hands on the ice, and in spite of the dull, overcast weather, I took a photograph to record the event.

He named the barren, icy desert Coats Land. Champagne and cigars were the order of the day. A fortnight later, Bruce recorded *Scotia*'s greatest depth at 2,764 fathoms. His soundings rewrote the maps of the Antarctic's oceans, being recognised in the Scotia Ridge and the Scotia Sea. Then *Scotia* dog-legged it home via some of the world's remotest spots: Gough Island, St Helena and Ascension Island. On 21 July, Bruce sailed up the Clyde to a hero's welcome, a message from King Edward VII and the award of the gold medal of the Royal Scottish Geographical Society.

Bruce is also remembered at the other end of the globe in the settlement of Brucebyen on Svalbard in the Norwegian Arctic. He made nine expeditions to Spitsbergen (Svalbard) between 1898 and 1920. He brought back a sample of coal from his third expedition, sponsored by Prince Albert of Monaco, and established the Scottish Spitsbergen Syndicate in 1909 to back his mining explorations. Before the outbreak of the First World War he annexed large parts of the island to establish mineral rights: at the time Spitsbergen was a no man's land claimed by both Britain and Norway. In 1919, the syndicate funded the building of the Brucebyen settlement, consisting of four large houses, all pre-fabricated in Scotland and numbered for ease of re-assembly. There were barracks for the workers and an outhouse. Bruce lived there for a time in 1920 shortly before his death. The syndicate was finally wound up in 1953, having failed to realise its commercial ambitions. Today, Brucebyen is protected by the Norwegian government as a cultural heritage site.

Scots were enthusiastic backers of other polar exploration. Donald Smith, 1st Lord Strathcona, the Scots-born Canadian financier and politician, was a patron of the Australasian Antarctic expedition of 1911 led by Douglas Mawson. The explorer recognised Smith's sponsorship by naming a peak in the interior of Antarctica Mount Strathcona.

Two wealthy Scottish industrialists left their names on the icy continent, thanks to their backing of Ernest Shackleton's expeditions. On his return from Scott's *Discovery* voyage of 1903, Shackleton was determined to mount his own assault on the unclaimed South Pole. In order to make ends meet after his marriage, he'd had a succession of jobs, including as a journalist and acting as Secretary of the Scottish Royal Geographical Society, and he worked briefly as a PR man for William Beardmore, owner of the vast Glasgow engineering empire. Beardmore took a liking to young Shackleton. He was the first subscriber to Shackleton's British Antarctic expedition of 1907–09.

After three years of hard struggle to raise funds, Shackleton set sail aboard the *Nimrod* bound for Antarctica. Having wintered in huts built on Ross Island, on 29 October 1908 he headed due south across the Ross Ice Shelf. By December, the party had passed Scott's furthest point south. Only four men attempted the barrier in their way to the Pole, as by then only four ponies had survived. Their route through the Transantarctic Mountains took them up the 140-mile-long Beardmore Glacier, named by Shackleton after his Glasgow backer. This was to be the most dangerous and risky part of the route. The smooth glacier surface concealed treacherous crevasses which claimed the life of their last pony and very nearly killed one of the men. On 27 December 1908, the party reached the windswept 10,000-foot-high polar plateau. A fortnight later, barely 100 miles short of the Pole, Shackleton decided to turn back after planting the Union Jack at 88° 23'. Had he been prepared to risk the lives of his team, Shackleton could have claimed the

Pole. The four men successfully reached the rest of their party on 4 March 1909.

Undeterred by the experience, Shackleton planned another expedition from 1914 to 1916, this time to cross the Antarctic continent. He wrote to Sir James Caird, the wealthy Dundee jute manufacturer and philanthropist, asking for a donation of £50. Captivated by the idea, Caird reached deep into his pockets. He made the privately financed trip on the *Endurance* possible by promising £10,000 and in the event donated £24,000, amounting to millions of pounds today.

In January 1915, Shackleton named the 'undulating barrier of ice-laden landspill, ending in cliffs from 10 ft to 200 ft high' linking Coats Land and Luitpold Land the Caird Coast. The coast was not far from the spot where the *Endurance* had become trapped in the ice and had sunk. Today, *James Caird* is better known as the name of the tiny lifeboat in which Shackleton and five companions made the 800-mile-journey to seek help.

James Wordie remained one of Scotland's unsung polar heroes until 1999, when the UK Antarctic Place-names Committee named Wordie Bay and the Wordie Ice Shelf after him. The shy, unassuming Glaswegian studied geology at Glasgow and Cambridge universities, where he met some of the survivors of Scott's last Antarctic expedition. Their tales fired Wordie's imagination and he volunteered for Ernest Shackleton's Endurance expedition of 1914-16 as chief scientific officer. Having survived four and a half months' confinement on Elephant Island while waiting to be rescued, Wordie had an appetite for more. His interest switched to the Arctic, and he went to Spitsbergen in 1919 and 1920 with William Speirs Bruce. In 1921, he made the first ascent of Mount Beerenberg on the desolate Norwegian island of Jan Mayen. Over the next 17 years he led five more Arctic expeditions, including voyages to East Greenland and

Baffin Bay. Wordie Bay in the Canadian Arctic is named after him.

His exploring days over, Wordie became chairman of the Scott Polar Research Institute for 18 years from 1937. During the Second World War, he was instrumental in the Naval Intelligence's top secret Operation Tabarin, which shaped British policy towards the Antarctic, the Falklands and South Georgia. He established the first permanent British base on the Antarctic continent and played a key role in Vivian Fuchs' ground-breaking crossing of Antarctica between 1955 and 1958. He also helped to plan the first ascent of Mount Everest in 1953. One of Wordie's 'landmarks' may not survive, however, as the Wordie Ice Shelf is fast disappearing due to climate change.

A 'Scottish' archipelago

Scottish explorers are associated with several islands throughout the world. Ross Island, which shelters Port Blair in the Andaman Islands in the Bay of Bengal, commemorates East India Company (EIC) marine surveyor Sir Daniel Ross. In the late eighteenth century the British government sought to establish a penal colony and a safe harbour. Lord Cornwallis, the Governor-General of India, asked Archibald Blair, whose name suggests at least some Scottish blood, to find a suitable location. Blair's report on the Andaman Islands was so favourable that he was invited to set up the settlement at Port Blair in 1788. Fellow surveyor and EIC employee Sir Daniel Ross chose Ross Island, strategically sited at the entrance to Port Blair harbour, as the location for the settlement's hospital. Ross was born in Jamaica, where his father Hercules Ross from Port Glasgow was busy making his fortune as a ship owner, trader and privateer.

Disease forced the abandonment of Port Blair and Ross's

settlement a decade later. The Indian Mutiny of 1857, however, resulted in the revival of plans for a penal colony, with
Ross Island being chosen as the headquarters of the operation
because of the availability of water. The first superintendent was
the Aberdonian James Pattison Walker, who set the prisoners to
clearing the jungle. His short regime was harsh, resulting in the
so-called 'Battle of Aberdeen', where escaped convicts joined
indigenous people in attacking the fort. Although the rebellion
was quashed by the might of guns against bows and arrows, it
made the British government think again and introduce a more
humane regime.

Known as the 'Paris of the East', Ross Island later became a
comfortable billet for British officers. In its heyday, social life
focused on the commissioner's bungalow, the officers' clubs,
the swimming pool and the Protestant church. Invaded by the
Japanese during the Second World War, the penal colony was
abolished when the Allies re-occupied the island in 1945. Today,
Ross Island lies in ruins, a curiosity for visitors.

The origin of the British name Falkland Islands for the
archipelago in the South Atlantic is undisputed. In 1690 Captain
John Strong of the *Welfare* landed to replenish his water supplies.
He named the stretch of water between the two main islands
'Falkland Sound' after Anthony Carey, 5th Viscount Falkland,
Treasurer to the Navy, financial supporter of Strong's voyage and
future First Lord of the Admiralty. Despite the name, however, the
link to Scotland is tenuous. An ancestor of Lord Falkland's, Henry
Carey, scion of an Oxfordshire family, was created first Viscount
Falkland and Lord Carye in the Scottish peerage in 1620. The
title and its descent to 'heirs male bearing the name of Carye' was
confirmed by a patent of naturalisation of 1627, as if he and his
heirs were natives of Scotland. English privateer Captain Woode
Rogers named the whole archipelago 'Falkland's Land' in 1708.

The islands remained uninhabited until the French founded a colony at Port Louis on East Falkland in 1764. After the British reasserted their claim in 1832, the government encouraged sheep rearing as a means of bringing prosperity to the islands. Many immigrants were Scottish shepherds, some later moving to southern Patagonia, Argentina, tempted by land grants in the province of Santa Cruz. Among them was William Halliday from Dumfriesshire, who settled with his family on the bank of the Rio Gallegos and founded one of the best known sheep stations in the province.

Some humbler Scots are honoured on the Falkland Islands map. The Purvis Glacier and Point Purvis on South Georgia record James Purvis, who served for seven years as an able sea-man and assistant cook on several ships sailing under the British government's Discovery investigations of the 1920s. The series of expeditions to the South Atlantic and beyond aimed to gather data on the biology of whales to set the management of com-mercial whale fishing on a more scientific footing. James Purvis must have been an exceptional crew member, as he was awarded a coveted Polar Medal; it is likely that he was a Scot, as the other linguistic landmark he left is Jock Point on the island's north coast.

'Scottish' islands become ever more present the icier the climate and the closer to Antarctica. The third largest of the Falkland Islands is named Weddell Island after Scottish sealer James Weddell. Weddell himself named the South Orkney Islands south of the Falklands. They lie at roughly the same latitude south (60°) as the Orkney Islands are north (59°). It is not known whether this influenced Weddell in his naming of them, and of the South Shetland Islands.

Weddell was born in Ostend in Belgium, where his father, a Lanarkshire upholsterer, had resorted because of his health. Although a seafarer by training, James was an explorer at heart. He persuaded Leith ship owner James Strachan to lend him his brig *Jane* for a sealing expedition in 1821. As Weddell was sponsored in part by the Admiralty, he named Cape Dundas after the First Lord, Robert Dundas, Second Viscount Melville of the Scottish political and legal dynasty. When William Speirs Bruce's Scotia expedition conducted the first proper survey of the South Orkneys, it was evident that mapmaking was not one of Weddell's skills.

Weddell followed his pursuit of seals, whales and adventure ever further southwards. With Admiralty backing, he was permitted to 'prosecute a search beyond the track of former navigators' should his search for seals prove unprofitable. Again he commanded the *Jane*, while fellow Scot Matthew Brisbane took charge of the *Beaufoy*. By mid-February 1823, the two ships had reached 74° 34' S, the furthest south that any explorer would reach until 1911. Despite sighting a few icebergs, however, Weddell decided that nothing but sea lay between him and the South Pole, and he turned back to pick up his search for seals. Had he sailed on for just two more days, he would have reached the future Coats Land.

Weddell continued his southern adventures narrowly surviving death by tying himself to a rock after his ship ran aground in a storm. He died in London in relative poverty and obscurity in 1834. His legacy was the Weddell seal and the Weddell Sea, renamed after him in 1900 and made famous as the sea in which Antarctic explorer Ernest Shackleton's ship *Endurance* became fatally trapped in the ice.

Dundee Island, at the northern tip of the Antarctic Peninsula, brings together several Scottish polar stars. With ice cliffs towering over the sea, the 2,000-foot-high island is almost permanently covered by snow and ice, Cape Purvis being its most prominent feature. Sir James Clark Ross, who named the Cape after a naval superior, discovered and roughly charted the island, spending

New Year's Day 1843 on shore. In 1892, a fleet of Dundee whalers sailed on an exploratory trip to the Antarctic, looking for whales. The young William Speirs Bruce was taken on as surgeon and naturalist. Thomas Robertson, the captain of the whaler *Active*, named the island after his ship's home port and the stretch of water between it and Joinville Island, the Firth of Tay.

From the seabed to the stars

Exploration has not been confined to land masses, whether continents or lonely atolls. The Challenger Deep in the western Pacific is the deepest known point in the world's oceans. At 36,070 feet below sea level, it is more than a mile deeper than Mount Everest is high.

The name reflects the Challenger expedition of 1872-76, which undertook the first systematic study of the deep oceans. It was a peculiarly Scottish affair, with Edinburgh graduate and professor of natural philosophy Charles Wyville Thomson as scientific leader and Canadian-born John Murray as naturalist. Much of the preparation took place in Edinburgh and at the end of the voyage the Challenger Office was established there, producing a 50-volume report of the expedition's findings.

The expedition answered three apparently simple questions: how deep are the oceans, what is the bottom of the deep ocean made of, and does life exist there? It succeeded for the first time ever in systematically sampling the deep seafloor, plotting the ocean's currents and temperatures, mapping the bottom deposits and outlining the contours of the ocean basins, including the discovery of the mid-Atlantic Ridge and the Mariana Trench in the Pacific east of the Philippines. The finding of 715 new genera and 4,717 new species of ocean life disproved once and for all that the deep oceans were barren and lifeless. In 1951, the

British survey ship *Challenger II*, named after the first expedition and captained by George Ritchie, who was born in Burnley of Scottish parents, discovered the deepest point of the Mariana Trench, which they named the Challenger Deep.

The expedition did not confine itself to the seabed. In the winter of 1873-74 it called in at the Kerguelen Islands, lying off Antarctica over 3,000 miles from the nearest population. The crew christened it Desolation Island. The naturalists on board were fascinated by the elephant seals, which they called Sea Elephants, already fast declining in numbers due to the predations of whalers. Hybrid names such as Ile Murray and Cap du Challenger reflect the French ownership of the archipelago. The highest mountain is the active volcano Mont Ross, named after the earlier explorer Sir James Clark Ross, who spent two months here taking measurements in his hunt for the South Magnetic Pole.

SCOTS AND THE STARS

Dorsa Geikie, a wrinkle ridge system on the Moon, is named after Scots geologist Archibald Geikie. Clackmannan is a crater on asteroid 253 Mathilde, while 243 Ida has a crater called Fingal – both named after famous caves. Craters on Mars include Ayr and Banff.

Simpelius, a lunar impact crater on the Moon, was named in 1651 by the Jesuit astronomer Giovanni Riccioli in honour of the Scots-born Jesuit mathematician Hugh Sempill, who headed the Royal Scots College in Madrid. Scots are honoured in the names of other lunar craters. They include James Gregory, the seventeenth-century astronomer; James Clerk Maxwell, the nineteenth-century physicist; John Napier, the sixteenth-century mathematician; and William Rankine, the nineteenth-century engineer.

Archieroy, the inner main belt asteroid (5806), discovered by a US astronomer in 1986, was named after Archie Roy, the Glaswegian-born professor of astronomy at Glasgow University.

V. Cassiopeiae was the first of 53 variable stars discovered by amateur Edinburgh astronomer Thomas Anderson in the 1890s. He also identified two well-known novae, the brightening of a white dwarf due to a massive nuclear explosion – Nova Aurigae and Nova Persei.

Alpha Centauri C., also known as Proxima Centauri, is one of the three major stars which make up the third brightest star system in the night sky, and of them is the closest to Earth at just over four light-years away. It was discovered in 1915 by Scottish astronomer Robert Innes, director of the Union Observatory in Johannesburg, South Africa.

Maxwell's Gap in planet Saturn's C ring is named after James Clerk Maxwell, the eminent Scottish physicist who deduced through mathematical equations in 1859 that Saturn's rings cannot be solid and must be made of 'an indefinite number of unconnected particles'.

2

The hallmark of trade

Trade was a precursor to putting down roots. Although Scots had a wide network of business contacts overseas from earliest times, trade as a driver to emigration took off on a large scale from the first half of the seventeenth century when it is estimated that up to 150,000 Scots were on the move from a total population of around a million.

The Scots move to Europe

The new Plantations of Ulster were created by the crown in the early seventeenth century from land confiscated from the defeated Gaelic clan chiefs. They offered good farmland as well as a culture not dissimilar to home, only a short sea crossing away from Ayrshire or Galloway. In the famine years of the 1690s in Scotland, Ulster also offered an escape from poverty and troubled politics. Scots left their mark where they settled through townland names. Some highlighted local natural features like a burn, brae, kirk or knowe, while others like Newtonstewart and Dunlopstown were a means of recording the owner's surname or, in the case of Scotchtown or Caledon, of making a statement about the family's identity.

Mainland Europe tended to attract young single men, thanks in part to well-established trading networks. A journey to the Baltic was shorter than to London, so Scandinavia, the Low Countries and the coastal regions of Eastern Europe were natural destinations for these restless adventurers. This was particularly true during the first half of the seventeenth century, when Sweden and Denmark held economic and military sway and were natural magnets for Scots on the make, whether as mercenaries or pedlars. There were 400 Scottish settlements in Poland and along the Prussian coast alone. The Scots integrated quickly into local society, leaving their stamp on local surnames rather than place names – Douglas, Chalmers, Forbes, Gordon and Reid.

A few place names survive. In Norway, Skottesteinen, the Scots stone on the approach to Nedstrand, was probably a by-product of the timber trade which the Scots dominated in the sixteenth and seventeenth centuries to the extent that the business was known as the *skottehandelen*, the Scotch trade. It was a barter system, Scottish skippers trading cereals for timber. Hjeltefjorden, the Shetland fjord, leading from the open sea to Bergen, attests to a centuries-old trade with the treeless Scottish islands.

Two suburbs of Gdansk in Poland – Szkoty Stare, or Altschottland, and Szkoty Nowe (Old and New Scotland) – reflect centuries of business and cultural exchange. Gdansk was the port of entry to Poland for many Scots. Some, such as Aberdeenshire traders Robert Gordon and 'Danzig' Willie Forbes, made their fortunes while countless young men headed out into the Polish countryside with pedlars' packs on their backs. In Poland, as in parts of Sweden and Denmark, the words *schotte* or *szot* were used to describe pedlars and commercial travellers.

Scotland's Empire

By the seventeenth century, Scots were also starting to look west. Nova Scotia, or New Scotland, was the brainchild of William

Alexander, Earl of Stirling. His poetry first brought him to the attention of King James VI and I, and he was soon a firm favourite at the court in London. Here he mingled with adventurers with ambitions to found English colonies overseas. He wanted to ensure that Scotland had its own slice of the action. Through the influence of the governor of Newfoundland, he was granted the north-west corner of the island, which he named Alexandria. He quickly moved on to more grandiose plans. In 1621, he persuaded the king to approach the newly formed Council of New England to grant land north of the Saint Croix River. It was named New Scotland to be upsides with New England.

Over the next six years, however, Alexander failed to recruit even one pioneer to settle the new land. In 1624, he published a marketing brochure entitled *An encouragement to colonies*, with a map dividing the territory into two provinces, Alexandria and Caledonia, and giving the main rivers the Scottish names, Clyde and Tweed. The king added his support by conferring the title of baronet on any Scot who would take up and settle a portion of land. There were no takers. He made a second offer, selling the titles in return for a payment to Alexander towards the settlers' upkeep. Although the king died four days later, his son, Charles I, was also supportive of the scheme. He renewed his father's charter, with provisions for the incorporation of Nova Scotia into Scotland and the creation of 150 baronets. Recipients were not required to travel to their recently acquired estates: all they had to do was to receive a handful of earth from the king's representative on what later became the esplanade of Edinburgh Castle. To this day, Canadians consider the esplanade to be Canadian territory.

By mid-1626, only 28 individuals had taken up the offer and Alexander was seriously out of pocket. Despite further royal backing, the figure had only risen to 85 when he was ordered to give up his settlement at Port Royal to the French in 1632. By now the king was desperately short of money, at odds with his parliament and keen to negotiate a settlement with the French, who had colonial ambitions in Canada. Indeed, one of the deterrents to attracting settlers to Nova Scotia had been a rival claim by the French, who had nominally occupied the land as Acadia. The sale of baronetcies degenerated into a money-raising scheme. Alexander died a broken man, with creditors hovering over his deathbed. His main achievements were to give the magnet of Scots emigration two centuries later its name and its flag: a saltire with the colours reversed, emblazoned with the royal arms of Scotland.

An even more ambitious attempt to found a trading colony came to an even more dramatic climax at the end of the century. New Caledonia, Panama, was the place that the Scots failed to put on the map. Even the isthmus between the Caribbean and the Pacific is today called the Isthmus of Panama rather than of Darien. Decades of warfare and exclusion from trade with the lucrative English colonies, compounded by years of famine, had brought Scotland to its knees in the late 1690s. Adventurer William Paterson, who had previously gone south to set up the Bank of England, came up with the answer – a scheme to revive trade by founding a Scottish colony. A sailor had told him of a paradise in Panama with rich land, a sheltered bay and friendly natives. It went by the name of Darien. Goods from the Pacific could be ferried across the isthmus and reloaded on to ships to cross the Atlantic, with the colony charging for the right to cross.

In 1695, the Company of Scotland Trading to Africa and the Indies was set up to raise money. The idea caught the public's imagination and, within weeks, wealthy landowners and small savers alike had invested £400,000 in the scheme. Five ships set sail from Leith on 4 July 1698, with 1,200 would-be settlers on board, of whom 70 died on the voyage. Only Paterson and the ship's commander knew the final destination. The emigrants lost nearly two months trying to build a settlement in what Paterson himself described as 'a mere morass, neither fit to be fortified nor planted, nor indeed for men to lie upon'. They then moved to a site which they called Fort St Andrew, which defended the dwellings of New Edinburgh. They encountered unfertile land, hostile Native American peoples, torrential rain, insects, unbearably humid weather, indiscipline, back-breaking work, hunger and disease, as well as a ban on trading with them imposed by King William III and the threat of attack by the Spanish. By spring 1699, an average of ten people a day were dying. The decision was taken to abandon the colony. Of the four ships that left Darien, only one made it back to Scotland, with less than 300 survivors on board.

Meanwhile, ignorant of the fate of the first expedition, the second set out in August 1699, with 1,302 emigrants on board three ships. This time 160 people died during the voyage. Arriving – ironically – on St Andrew's Day, the new settlers started to rebuild New Edinburgh but were faced with the same intractable problems. Foolishly, they attacked the Spanish, provoking them into besieging Fort St Andrew, which was forced to surrender in March 1700. The colonists were allowed to leave, but few made it back to Scotland. New Caledonia was abandoned to the jungle and the Darien Scheme hastened the union between Scotland and England in 1707.

Yet some colonists chose to remain in America rather than face the hazardous crossing back to Scotland, where survivors were made to feel like pariahs. One such colonist was Archibald Stobo, who was shipwrecked off South Carolina on the *Rising Sun*. He made Charleston his home and set up the First (Scots) Presbyterian Church in 1731, one of the earliest in the South.

The church still celebrates Scottish Heritage Sunday each September, with kilts, bagpipes and the Kirkin' o' the Tartan.

Lands of sugar, tobacco and rum

The Act of Union of 1707 finally gave Scots adventurers a place in the sun, opening up the increasingly lucrative English colonies to trade, especially in sugar and tobacco. Scots were not slow to take advantage. They found an existing community of Scots in the Caribbean islands who had come over as labourers; however, plantation owners found that it was cheaper to import slaves from Africa.

One of the earliest to realise the potential of Jamaica was Col John Campbell from Inveraray, who had previously sailed with the Darien expedition. Blaming the English for its failure and declaring that he would never return to Scotland while it was considering Union, he set up as a sugar planter on the Black River, the first of a long dynasty of Campbell planters.

An immediate task for landowners like Campbell was to survey their property. Born in Shetland in 1756, James Robertson became Jamaica's most famous surveyor. He and his fellow Scots surveyors were influential in dividing the island into sugar and slave plantations, many of which acquired Scottish names – Glasgow, Argyle, Glen Islay, Dundee, Fort William, Montrose, Roxbro, Dumbarton, Old Monklands and Mount Stewart.

By 1750, Scots accounted for one-third of Jamaica's white population, with place names such as Culloden and Craigie reflecting their roots. Young Scots fortune-hunters rushed to offer their services as slave masters, doctors and administrators. Only promising sales of his poetry dissuaded Robert Burns from heading to Jamaica: he had already purchased his ticket. Jamaica proved particularly attractive to young men from the north-east, who often arrived in the Caribbean without land or money. If they did well, they bought a plantation (or more than one), managed it, sold it on and retired to Scotland to live the life of the landed gentry.

One such planter was Aberdonian Alexander Forbes, who named his large sugar plantation in St Elizabeth Parish Aberdeen. With fellow Scot Alexander Donaldson, he also ran a cotton trading company with an office in Port-au-Prince, in the French colony of Saint-Domingue. A slave revolt at the turn of the seventeenth century resulted in the creation of Haiti, the world's oldest black nation. Forbes did much to support the refugees and, after emancipation in 1838, the former slaves founded their own town on the edge of the estate, naming it Aberdeen. Other Jamaican plantations with north-east connections included the Monymusk Estate of the Grants of Monymusk; the Burn Estate of John Shand, who owned the Burn near Fettercairn; and the Dalvey Estate of Sir Alexander Grant of Dalvey near Forres.

Jamaica also has its own Edinburgh Castle, an estate with a now ruined two-storey tower house in a remote part of St Ann's Parish. It was built in the 1760s by Lewis Hutchinson, a Scot who had some medical training. Initially earning a living rustling his neighbours' cattle, he soon turned to even darker pursuits and has a lasting place in the island's history as its earliest recorded serial killer. 'The mad doctor' would kill travellers passing by the lonely spot with a single shot, rob them of their belongings and force his slaves to throw their bodies in a sinkhole on the estate. He sometimes entertained his guests before dispatching them. Emboldened by his killing spree, Hutchinson shot a neighbour and a soldier in view of a fellow colonist. Failing to escape by ship, he was captured, tried and hanged at the Spanish Town Gallows in 1773. The final death toll will never be known, although a search of Edinburgh Castle after his arrest revealed 43 watches and piles of clothing.

By 1800, Jamaica had 300,000 slaves, overseen by 10,000 Scots and 10,000 Englishmen. Wealthy whites took up residence in St Andrew Parish. In the shadow of the parish's cool, misty Blue Mountains, Dr Colin McClarty from Campbeltown, Argyllshire, opened the first coffee plantation, the Clydesdale Estate, from which the region takes its name, in the late eighteenth century. He'd originally planned a short visit but fell in love with the island and decided to stay. Other farmers followed his example. Now derelict, the Clydesdale coffee factory retains its drying patios and water wheel. The nearby Mavis Bank village is centred on its Blue Mountain coffee factory, the largest on the island. The origin of its name is obscure. The assumption that it was named after Mavisbank House, built by leading Scottish Enlightenment figure Sir John Clerk of Penicuik in the 1720s, is possible, as various members of the Clerk family emigrated to Jamaica.

Barbados, too, had its St Andrew Parish but also, within it, Scotland itself. During the colonial period, the hills and fields of the area overlooked by the island's highest peak, Mount Hillaby, reminded colonists of home. The island's coat of arms carries the cross of St Andrew in the shape of stalks of sugar cane, while a stone on the Knapdale Estate in St Ann Parish bears the coat of arms of its first owner, Duncan Campbell, a descendant of the first Duke of Argyll.

Sometimes plantation owners chose to give their estates their own names. Aberdonian doctor James Clark was one such owner. Having emigrated to Dominica about 1770, he is known to have had a 40-year relationship with an African-European woman known as Mary. He amassed a fortune, which allowed him to purchase several coffee and sugar plantations, including one that is still known as the Clark Hall Estate. He never lost touch with the British medical establishment, publishing a treatise on yellow fever in 1797. Jonathan Troup, a young fellow Aberdonian doctor serving in Dominica, wrote in his journal in 1789: 'Dr Clark has about 50 Negroes employed – he makes very great profits by them.' He recalled seeing 'Dr Clark's Negro with a chain and collar of iron round his neck. Though he is strong, the weight made him bleed at nose and mouth.' James Laing was one of Clark's closest friends and yet another Aberdeenshire doctor. His fortune from his coffee plantations encouraged his nephew, William Bremner, to buy a plantation and name it the Aberdeen Estate.

Slaves were treated as personal property, the plantation owner choosing how to name the individual who, during the journey from Africa, had only borne a number. About 15 per cent of slaves in Jamaica, almost exclusively male, were named after British towns or other places that had associations for the owner. Scottish plantation owners followed the custom. William McDowall, who owned sugar plantations in Nevis and St Kitts in the early eighteenth century, gave his slaves names such as Paisley, Craigends and Kilbarchan. A government slave census of 1817 recorded almost 300 slaves named Aberdeen throughout the British West Indies.

Scots also settled in non-British colonies such as 'Demerary', now part of Guyana but for most of the eighteenth century owned by the Dutch. Sugar plantations included Edinburgh, Glasgow, Strathspey, Perth, Dundee, Caledonia, Aberdeen, Dunkeld, Montrose, and Annandale, which today survive as the names of villages, having been retained after the plantations were broken up and farmed by former slaves.

Tobacco took enterprising Scots to the mainland plantations of America. Ironically, Jamestown, the birthplace of the tobacco industry, had been named after the Scottish king, James VI and I, who inveighed against 'this filthy novelty' as early as 1604. One such entrepreneur, John Graham, named his new settlement after his birthplace. The town seal of Dumfries, Virginia, features the two plants that tell his story – the thistle and the tobacco leaf. A downturn in his family's fortunes, which forced them to sell their estate in Scotland, may have forced Graham, born in 1711, to seek a better life. He may have been inspired by the sight of ships heading for Virginia in the dock. In the 1730s Dumfries had ten or twelve ships engaged in the tobacco trade and was known as 'the Scottish Liverpool'.

Emigrating to Virginia in 1739, Graham established a business exporting tobacco and shipping in goods required on the plantations. A month after his marriage, his wife died, but he soldiered on, and by 1744 he was in a position to buy land on the south side of Quantico Creek, Prince William County. He built tobacco warehouses on the land, known today as Graham Park. His Graham Park Plantation was a self-sustained operation, with its own craftsmen as well as slaves or indentured servants.

After much political manoeuvring, in 1749 the legislature in Williamsburg granted a charter for a town to be formed on Quantico Creek on land donated by Graham, one of the town's seven trustees. Today, Dumfries is the oldest continuously chartered town in Virginia. By the mid-1750s, Graham was an established figure. Remarriage came with the gift of a position as county clerk inherited from his new father-in-law, assuring him a place among Virginia's aristocracy. He moved into the business of building river boats and the hobby of horse racing. By the time of his death in 1787, he had laid down a Virginian dynasty, one of his sons becoming Secretary of War under Presidents Madison and Monroe.

One Virginian plantation had to wait until its fortunes changed before it acquired a Scottish name. A Col William Fitzhugh created Ravensworth, one of the largest tobacco plantations in Northern Virginia, in 1685. Over time his descendants sold off parcels of land, and by 1830 the turnpike road between Fairfax and Alexandria crossed the plantation and small farms rather than fields of tobacco plants dominated the landscape. The area was now known as Annandale after the river valley in Dumfriesshire.

Scots were also involved in setting up a very different type of plantation on an island on the other side of the world – tea in Sri Lanka. Again many named their plantations after places back home – Aberdeen, Balmoral, Blair Atholl, Braemar, Braemore, Caledonia, Clyde, Clydesdale, Cullen, Culloden, Dalhousie, Dunbar, Dunkeld, Elgin, Glasgow, Gleneagles, Goatfell, Highland, Iona, Kinross, Kirkoswald, Lammermoor, Liddesdale, Macduff, Midlothian, Morar, Moray, Newburgh, Perth, Portree, Sanquhar, St Andrews, Strathspey, Sutherland, Tillicoultry, Urie and Ythanside.

It was only around 1870, after blight had destroyed the coffee crop, Sri Lanka's main export, that planters switched to tea, thanks largely to two Scots. In 1851, 16-year-old James Taylor had signed on as an assistant supervisor on a coffee plantation: he never saw his native land again. He set up the first tea 'factory' on the island and in 1872 he invented a machine for rolling leaves. His first tea reached the London auctions three years later. By the time of his death in 1892 the Ceylon tea industry was largely owned by British capital and Ceylon had largely replaced China tea as the fashionable afternoon drink.

Glaswegian Thomas Lipton helped to turn tea into the everyday cuppa. In 1890, already a millionaire from his grocery empire, Lipton paid a visit to Sri Lanka. Distrustful of middlemen, he bought four plantations, allowing him to control quality and price. Sitting under a canopy on the edge of a cliff in the misty mountains above Haputale, Lipton would survey his estates 6,000 feet below, cup of tea in hand, and boast: 'Everything that you can see from here is mine.' His brightly coloured packets carried the message: 'Straight from the tea gardens to the tea pot'. Today, Sri Lanka is among the world's largest exporters of tea.

Opening up the Far North

While the south turned plants into gold, in the far north, the beaver was turned into silver, through the great trading empires of the Hudson's Bay Company (HBC) and the North West Company (NWC). The trade was essentially founded on fashion: the pelt of the beaver was shaved, steamed, felted and brushed to make a variety of hats, from the topper to the naval cocked hat. Resilient and malleable beaver felt was only eclipsed in the late nineteenth century when fashion switched to silk: by this time, the Canadian beaver had been hunted almost to extinction.

Both companies were largely staffed by Scots. By the end of the eighteenth century more than three-quarters of HBC staff employed overseas were Orcadians. The company found them to be hardy, resourceful, loyal and less susceptible to drink and First Nation women than the London slum dwellers whom they had initially employed. Highlanders dominated the NWC's payroll, especially in the lower ranks as clerks and servants.

Once the wilderness areas of Canada had been explored and extraction routes identified, the next step was to establish a network of trading posts. One of the most famous of these was Fort William, Ontario. The William in question was a poor Highlander, William McGillivray, who was born in 1764 at Dunlichty in Inverness-shire. When his uncle, Simon McTavish, who had been living in North America for the past 12 years, visited the family in 1776 he discovered that William's parents could not afford to educate all of their six children. McTavish's promise to finance William and his brother Duncan through secondary education proved a shrewd investment. In 1784, he brought William to Montreal and hired him to work for the NWC. William worked his way up to head the whole organisation from 1804 to 1821. Along the way, around 1790, he 'married' a mixed-blood woman named Susan, with whom he had three sons and a daughter. A decade later, having reached the top, he officially married Magdalen McDonald in London.

After abandoning their trading post at Grand Portage, which McGillivray had managed in the 1790s, the Nor'Westers established a new post on the mouth of the Kaministiquia River as it enters Lake Superior. The post was named Fort William in 1807. It became the key midway trans-shipment point for 'winterers' paddling from the west carrying furs, and 'pork eaters' coming from the east bearing trade goods and supplies. They met at the annual Great Rendezvous. Peaceful Fort William became the centre of frenzied activity as hundreds of voyageurs, clerks, partners and agents arrived. Tons of furs were sorted, cleaned and re-packed for shipment to Montreal. Supplies from the east were loaded for distribution to the various 'departments' in the western interior.

Incorporated as a city in 1907, Fort William no longer exists, it having been amalgamated with other population centres to form the new city of Thunder Bay in 1970. Today, the Great Rendezvous is recreated each July when hundreds of period re-enactors from throughout North America gather at Fort William Historical Park to reawaken the spirit of the fur trade.

A career with the HBC offered an opportunity of a lifetime for impoverished Scots. Born on the Orkney island of South Ronaldsay around 1739, William Tomison was responsible for naming Canada's most northerly city, Edmonton. Tales of adventure heard on the quays of Stromness may have inspired the lad, who had no formal education, to sign on as a labourer with the HBC, whose operations in Western Canada he was destined to lead from 1778 to 1810. He trailblazed a path that many of his fellow islanders were to follow.

Being sent to winter with the First Nation people gave Tomison an insight into their customs and languages which few of his fellow employees could match. He gained a reputation at HQ for his knowledge of the fur trade and for being 'greatly beloved by the Natives'. Promoted in 1778 as inland master, he established a chain of new trading posts to compete with rival Canadian interests. One of these was Fort Edmonton, which he set up in 1795. He named it Edmonton after an estate in England owned by the company's deputy governor, Sir James Winter Lake.

By now Tomison's career was showing signs of strain. The isolation of the inland posts had confirmed his natural preference for a solitary and Spartan existence. He showed little interest in socialising with his fellow officers, who accused him of meanness and rigidity as a manager. In poor health and out of touch with a new generation of officers, in 1810 Tomison finally returned to his native South Ronaldsay, where he funded a free school for future generations to benefit from the formal education of which poverty had deprived him.

Created in 1822 as an HBC trading post at the confluence of the Mackenzie and Liard rivers, Fort Simpson, Northern Territories, reflects the career of another rags-to-riches fur trader. George Simpson was born out of wedlock near Loch Broom in Wester Ross around 1787. He left Scotland as a teenager to work in his uncle's sugar-broking firm in London. Through his uncle's business connections, Simpson found himself catapulted to fame, much to his own surprise, as temporary governor-in-chief to the HBC in 1820. He had to learn the fur trade fast.

He was immediately faced with a crisis, as relations between the HBC and the NWC had reached a state of intermittent violence. He successfully helped to negotiate the amalgamation of the two companies in 1821 and was rewarded with the post of governorship of the northern department, which stretched from Rainy Lake, Ontario, to the Pacific coast. Five years later he was appointed chief of the whole empire. Simpson ruled with a canny if sometimes autocratic hand. Although on occasion cold-hearted, he was considered to be efficient and fair, and a peacemaker. He appreciated the risks of over-trapping, instructing traders to move on until beaver populations were restored.

George Simpson was a born explorer, using the excuse of tours of duty to escape into the wilderness: 'All my ailments vanish as soon as I seat myself in a canoe.' In 1824, he abandoned a planned trip to London to look for a wife, preferring to explore the potential of the Columbia River to act as a buffer to keep out rival American fur traders. Setting out in a light canoe manned by eight men and a First Nation guide, he reached Fort George, Oregon, 84 days later, breaking the record from Hudson Bay to the Pacific by 20 days.

In his 40-year career, Simpson rarely failed to make at least one arduous journey annually: in 1828, his hopes of making the Fraser River a fur-trade route were almost literally dashed thanks to the river's rapids and whirlpools. In 1841–42, he made a world trip, partly on the pretext of negotiations with the Russians and the Americans over the fur trade. Sailing from London, he crossed North America by horse and canoe, then sailed to Hawaii, where the HBC had established an agency trading timber, fish and flour for local products. Returning to Sitka in Alaska, he completed his 19-month journey back to London via Siberia and St Petersburg. Arguably, he was the first person to circumnavigate the globe by land. It was probably with a twinge of envy that he supported the Arctic expedition of Peter Warren Dease and his cousin, Thomas Simpson. His support and his importance as a businessman earned him a knighthood in 1841.

Now a popular kayaking stop, Fort Simpson remained a 'company town' until 1910. Simpson is also honoured in Simpson's Falls on the Peace River, the Simpson Pass on the border of Alberta and British Columbia, and Cape George Simpson, named in his honour by his explorer cousin, Thomas.

Simpson's official wife also earned her place in history in Fort Frances, Ontario, the oldest European settlement west of Lake Superior. When in his forties, he married his first cousin, 18-year-old Frances Simpson, by whom he had five children. By then he had already fathered at least five children in a series of relationships with mixed-blood women. These relationships were formalised in the practice engaged in by many fur traders known as marriage *à la façon du pays*. Although there was no obligation on the man to provide for his 'wife', if they separated, the normal custom was to make some such provision. Simpson was the exception, disposing of his partners with little sentiment and excluding any mixed-blood women from his household with, perhaps unsurprisingly, the full support of Frances. In 1830, the Simpsons paid an official visit to the HBC's permanent fur-trading post, Lac La Pluie, on the Rainy River. As was his custom on such visits, he insisted that a piper played Highland tunes. Later that year Lac La Pluie became Fort Frances to honour the VIP lady.

Whereas the legacy of explorer Sir Alexander Mackenzie, who discovered Canada's largest river system, is well known, that of his fur-trader cousin Donald is less so, the McKenzie River, Oregon: it lacks the 'a' of its more famous counterpart, as Donald spelled his name with a 'Mc' while Alexander favoured 'Mac'. Born in Achnaclerach, near Contin in Ross and Cromarty, in 1783, 21-stone Donald McKenzie was a larger-than-life character in more ways than one. His agility defied his weight and earned him the nickname 'perpetual motion McKenzie'. Destined for the ministry, he escaped his fate by emigrating to Canada to seek adventure. He joined the NWC, where his brother, the future Sir Roderick McKenzie, was already installed.

After ten years as a fur trader, McKenzie was offered a partnership by John Jacob Astor, founder of the Astor dynasty and America's first multi-millionaire, in his newly formed Pacific Fur Company. He was dispatched as part of an overland party to set up a trading post at the mouth of the Columbia River in 1812. Ready for further adventures, he set out to explore the Willamette Valley. His party paddled upstream to the point where the Willamette forks into three branches. The first fork still bears his name. He enthused about the river, not only for being 'delightful beyond expression' but also for the number of beaver on its banks, which he believed to exceed anything yet found on the continent. He made a fortune as a fur trader, being nicknamed 'King of the Northwest'. After serving as governor of the Red River Settlement in the mid-1820s, he retired to New York State.

The Wild West

As pioneers pushed ever westwards through the United States, the wide, empty plains offered opportunities for cattle ranching. Here the Scots were active not only as ranchers but as investors in the emerging cattle industry that fed the industrial cities of the north. The first large joint stock venture in cattle ranching in Texas, the Prairie Cattle Company Ltd, was based in Edinburgh, although much of its capital came from Dundee. It is estimated that at one time three-quarters of overseas investment in US ranching came from Scotland, much of it from smaller investors who were attracted by the sales talk of the 'beef bonanza' promoters.

Investment led to ownership and two of the most famous ranches have direct links back to Scotland. The now vanished township of Aberdeen was once a hub of Texas ranching country and the base of the Rocking Chair Ranch Company. The 7th Earl of Aberdeen and his brother-in-law, Sir Edward Marjoribanks, bought the company and planned to develop its vast landholdings along the lines of a great country estate. In 1889, they laid out the town of Aberdeen as the nucleus of the ranch, which a young relative of Marjoribanks was appointed to manage. 'The Honourable Archie' soon became the laughing stock of local cowboys, spending most of his time in saloons and gambling dens, and being taken for a ride by rustlers. When the titled owners paid an unexpected visit to Aberdeen and requested a cattle census, the same cattle were driven around a hill several times to increase the count. The ranch was finally sold in 1896 and just over 50 years later the last Aberdeen resident moved away.

With a current population of more than 600, Murdo, South Dakota, has fared rather better than Aberdeen. It takes its name from the ranch manager, Murdo Mackenzie, the son of a tenant farmer from Edderton in Easter Ross. After training as a land manager, he was recruited in 1885 by the Prairie Cattle Company to run two ranching empires from a base in Trinidad, Colorado. Five years later he was appointed to run the Matador Land and Cattle Company of Dundee, the longest lived of the Scottish-owned investment vehicles in cattle ranching. The Matador had been badly affected by a slump following disastrous snow storms and floods. Mackenzie did much to improve its fortunes by reducing herd numbers and improving stock quality. After showing that Texas-born two-year-olds who were wintered on northern grass commanded top prices, he became founding president of the American Stock Growers Association. After a sojourn in São Paulo stocking and managing ten million acres for the Brazil

Land, Cattle and Packing Company, he returned to the Matador in 1918, his son taking over when he retired in 1937. When the Matador was wound up in 1951, as the land was close to an oil strike, the shares sold at 30 times the original price, excluding inflation.

Several townships in the west still bear names associated with Scots ranching pioneers. Philip, South Dakota, is named after the rancher James 'Scotty' Philip. He was born in 1858 on a farm outside Dallas, Moray. As a boy, Philip was an avid reader of tales of the American frontier, whose lurid descriptions of death, daring and untold riches often owed more to fiction than to fact. Fired by the possibilities of adventure, Philip emigrated, aged 15, to follow in the footsteps of his older brother, George, who had settled at Victoria, Kansas.

Life in Victoria turned out to be a disappointment, with long hours and a succession of menial jobs. Reading started Philip dreaming again, but this time it was newspaper accounts of the discovery of gold in the Black Hills. So he packed his bags, ending up in Cheyenne, Wyoming, where once more he was thwarted. He was thrown out of the Black Hills three times by US government troops patrolling the area to defuse conflicts between gold miners and First Nation people, who regarded the hills as sacred.

After a series of jobs, which included working as a cowboy at Fort Robinson, Philip decided that ranching was the life for him. He saved up for a team of mules and a wagon to haul freight, and started to build up his herd. His business turned out to be very lucrative, and after several moves he finally put down roots on a ranch at the mouth of the Grindstone Creek along the Bad River. With a neighbour, he established a post office and named it Philip.

He also benefitted from his marriage to Cheyenne Indian Sarah Larrabee. At the time Philip was on a reservation where white men could not run cattle unless they had a Native American wife. By the time the area was opened up to white settlers in 1898, Philip had acquired a vast acreage of land.

Philip has also earned his place in history as 'the man who saved the buffalo'. He became friendly with one Pete Dupree who reared buffalo, by now almost hunted to extinction on the Grand River. After Dupree's death, Philip purchased the herd and in 1901 drove the 50-plus head of buffalo to an enclosed pasture that he had built for the purpose along the Missouri River. In time, the herd grew to nearly a thousand beasts, the world's largest of its day. Progeny would later stock national and state parks throughout the United States.

In 1911, Philip, a popular and respected figure throughout the West, died suddenly. People travelled for three days to attend his funeral, where bankers and ranchers mingled with cowboys and Native Americans. It is even claimed that the buffalo came down from the hills to pay their last respects. To this day, residents of Philip are proud of their founder. School children have adopted 'Scotty' as a mascot and are known as the 'Mighty Philip Scotties'.

As a teenager, James 'Scotty' Philip may have found his stay in Victoria, Kansas, less than exciting, although he must have known about its founder, fellow Scot George Grant. Grant introduced the first Aberdeen Angus cattle to America when he transported four bulls to the Kansas Prairie in 1873. After a successful career as a silk merchant, his vision was to found a colony of wealthy stock-raisers from Britain. He named his settlement Victoria in a display of loyalty to his Queen. The four Angus bulls, probably from the herd of George Brown of Westertown, Fochabers, made a lasting impression on the US cattle industry. Forward-thinking Grant crossed some of his bulls with native Texas longhorn cows. The first great herds of Angus beef cattle in America were built up by purchasing stock directly from Scotland. Twelve hundred cattle alone were imported, mostly to the Midwest, between 1878 and 1883. Early owners, in turn, helped start other herds. Today, there is a memorial to Grant funded by several Aberdeen Angus cattle breeders' societies.

Getting cattle to market and organising onward shipment to the north involved the creation of cowboy cattle trails through vast expanses of open countryside. The most famous of these is the Chisholm Trail, Oklahoma, named after Jesse Chisholm, the half-Scots, half-Cherokee fur and Texas cattle trader, who marked out some of the route as a freight wagon trail in 1864. Although his route used paths established by the Native Americans long since, from 1865 it became known as Chisholm's trail, cattlemen later adding 'the' and dropping the apostrophe 's'. Illinois cattle buyer Joseph G. McCoy extended the trail to his vast new stock-yards at the railhead of Abilene for onward travel to the slaughter houses of cities such as Chicago. Drovers started to christen the entire trail from south Texas to north-east Kansas 'the Chisholm'. In 1892, journalist Charles Moreau Harger wrote the book *Cattle Trails of the Prairies* in which he described the Chisholm:

> From two hundred to four hundred yards wide, beaten into the bare earth, it reached over hill and through val-ley for over six hundred miles, a chocolate band amid the green prairies, uniting the North and the South. Bleaching skulls and skeletons of weary brutes who had perished on the journey gleamed along its borders, and here and there was a low mound showing where some cowboy had literally 'died with his boots on'.

The Chisholm Trail presented other opportunities for enter-prising Scots. After learning that an extension of the Chicago, Rock Island and Pacific Railroad was being built from Kansas to Texas, Scotsman William Duncan emigrated with his family to create a trading post, which he named Duncan, Oklahoma, at the intersection of the north–south Chisholm Trail and the east–west military passage between Fort Arbuckle and Fort Sill. The date of the arrival of the first train on 27 June 1892 is the official birthday of the town. Although its roots lie in cattle, Duncan's main claim to fame is as the birthplace of the Halliburton Corporation. After perfecting a new method of cementing oil wells, making production easier and more profitable, Erle P. Halliburton established the New Method Oil Well Cementing Company in Duncan in 1919.

The wide open spaces of Argentina were also ranching country. Some of the strong community of Scottish merchants in Buenos Aires branched out, treating land ownership as an investment. They were joined by adventurous young Scots with a farming background, who emigrated in the hope of making a fortune on the pampas by running cattle or sheep. John Parish Robertson even attempted to set up a Scottish colony. Aged only 14, Robertson left Scotland to make his fortune. With his brother William, he set up a trading house with dealings in Paraguay and Argentina, and bought land at Santa Catalina, Buenos Aires County, from fellow Scots, the Gibson Brothers. The land became home to the Monte Grande colony of 250 Scots, who had set sail from Leith in the *Symmetry* in 1825. Their bard Tam o' Stirling described their arrival in Buenos Aires:

> The Symmetry anchored, boats gathered around them,
> While jabbering foreigners their luggage received,
> The Babel o' tongues was enough to confound them.
> But naebody understood Scotch, they perceived.

Although the colony did not thrive and the settlers scattered, it left a lasting legacy. One of its first ministers, William Brown from Leuchars, founded the St Andrew Scots School in Buenos

Aires to preserve the Scots language, religion and culture: the school still operates today bilingually.

Because Scots owners of *estancias* retained their Spanish titles, Scottish names on the map of Argentina are sparse. One exception is the small village of Nueva Escocia in the region of Entre Rios.

Both government and individual estate owners promoted emigration schemes in the late nineteenth century. A group largely made up of Highlanders – Macdonalds, McNeills, Sinclairs, Buchanans and Frasers – took up plots of land at the Colonia Nueva Escocia. The Reverend Lachlan McNeill from Kilmun in Argyllshire had a parish stretching for 300 miles on either side of the River Uruguay. He held services at his many preaching stations in both English and Gaelic. Some colonists prospered and established their own *estancias*, giving them names such as Clyde, Kintail and Caledonia.

British interests dominated in the expansion of the rail network from the late nineteenth century to bring agricultural produce to market. Many Scots found employment as engineers, contractors and train drivers. The Central Argentine Railroad was built in the 1860s to link several cities, including Buenos Aires with Córdoba. The President decided that 'Dead Friar' was not a fitting name for one of the stations and so renamed it Bell Ville. The pun not only suggested an attractive location but also honoured two ranching settlers, Anthony and Richard Bell from Dunbar. Munro, in Buenos Aires County, takes its name from Duncan Mackay Munro, born in Inverness in 1845, the manager of the Ferrocarril Córdoba Central line. He had already named neighbouring Villa Adelina in 1909 after his favourite granddaughter.

The Far South

Scots were making their mark and money in the Far South as

well as in the Far North, and again it was exploitation of wildlife that encouraged them to settle. Killing seals for their fur, and whales for their meat, oil and even stays for corsets was big business in the nineteenth century.

Stewart Island, New Zealand, is the country's southernmost island. It takes its name from Scots-born Captain William W. Stewart. After serving with the Royal Navy and possibly as a privateer, he set up in business as a seal trader in the Bass Strait around 1797. A decade later saw him as first officer on the *Pegasus* when it visited New Zealand waters. The reason for the voyage has never satisfactorily been explained. Stewart followed Captain Cook in charting the coastline, proving that what he named Stewart Island was in fact an island and demonstrating considerable skill as a hydrographer.

Little is known of his movements thereafter until 1824, when he returned to Britain to promote the establishment of a timber, flax and trading station at Stewart Island. The settlement failed, although he continued to live there, becoming the subject of many sealers' tales. Given Stewart's larger-than-life character, there is even a question mark over whether he was the same William Stewart who charted the island – had he simply claimed the honour for himself? The island's seal colonies were decimated between 1810 and 1820. Six years later William Stewart, or possibly yet another individual with the same name, landed a group of boat-builders at Pegasus Harbour. They built a whaling schooner, the *Joseph Weller*, which is one of the first vessels recorded in the New Zealand Shipping Register.

Several place names on Stewart Island are associated with Scotland. Oban is its main settlement and Ulva Island protects Paterson Inlet in the same way that Ulva guards the entrance to Loch na Keal on Mull. To the south-west, Long Island is also known as Jura. In 1872, Orcadian Charles Traill established the region's first post office in Post Office Bay, Ulva Island. He used to raise a flag to alert the scattered communities to the arrival of the mail boat. The presence of the post office meant that Ulva Island became a social meeting place for locals, who would dress in their finery to pick up the mail and exchange gossip. Charles and his brother, Walter, planted some of the exotics which still grow among the native forest trees, contributing to Stewart Island's present status as New Zealand's first nature reserve.

One of the tall tales told about William Stewart was that he took Jacobite Prince Charles Edward Stuart's daughter, Charlotte, to Campbell Island, over 400 miles south of mainland New Zealand. This inhospitable island on the edge of Antarctica was discovered in 1810 by Captain Frederick Hasselborough of the *Perseverance*, a brig owned by Campbell & Co. of Sydney. Robert Campbell, the founder of the shipbuilding and trading firm, was born in Greenock in 1769. He worked in his brother's trading house in Calcutta before establishing his own business empire in Sydney. Usually the whereabouts of new sealing grounds was a trade secret, but in the case of Campbell Island the news leaked and the seal population was rapidly wiped out. Thereafter the island became a whaling station. The scientific expedition of 1840–42, led by Scot James Clark Ross, called in at Campbell Island, where the naturalists on board compiled the first plant and animal inventories.

Today, Campbell Island is uninhabited apart from periodic visits by scientific and conservation groups. The island made the international news headlines in 1992 when a single-engine helicopter made the world's longest rescue flight to come to the aid of a meteorologist who had been attacked by a shark while swimming off the island. It made the news again in 2001 when the New Zealand government embarked on the world's most ambitious rat eradication programme of its time – the unwanted legacy of Campbell's *Perseverance*.

At one time the seas around the island of South Georgia in the South Atlantic teemed with whales. Although the Dundee Antarctic expedition of 1892–93 concluded that whaling in Antarctic seas was not a viable economic proposition, improvements in equipment led to the emergence of a thriving industry. Initially only the blubber was taken and the discarded carcasses littered the beaches. By 1912, seven whaling stations had been established and South Georgia became known as the southern capital of whaling. Scottish investment switched from Dundee to Leith, and in particular to the whaling companies owned by Christian Salvesen & Co. The name is remembered in the jagged peaks of the Salvesen Range. From 1909 to 1965, a Salvesen subsidiary, the South Georgia Co., operated a factory at Leith Harbour. The largest of its whaling stations, this huge complex had its own generating stations, boiling plants, dormitories and even a hospital. Its history had an unusual final chapter. Argentinean merchant Constantino Davidoff had arranged with Christian Salvesen to extract scrap metals from Leith and other whaling stations. His unauthorised landing on South Georgia at the end of 1981 led to a formal complaint by the British Ambassador to Argentina, the prelude to the Falklands War.

Leith Harbour lay in Stromness Bay, probably named around 1909 by a whaling crew. Whalers had traditionally called in at Stromness on Orkney to recruit men and collect stores. It was here that Ernest Shackleton, Frank Worsley and Tom Crean arrived on 20 May 1916 after their heroic voyage from the Antarctic. Today, 100,000 king penguins breed on the gravel beach of St Andrews Bay.

'There's gold in them thar hills'

The lure of gold during the nineteenth-century gold rushes led to concentrations of Scots and Scottish place names in California, Yukon, Victoria, New South Wales and the Transvaal in South Africa.

In 1860, the discovery of gold nearby turned a sleepy Australian backwater into the 'Wahgunyah Rush'. The Star Hotel on the corner of Argyle Street quenched the thirsts of thousands of prospectors. The story goes that over a few drinks the locals were debating the need for a name for the rapidly expanding community. David G. Hamilton suggested if the Star's proprietor, John A. Wallace, was prepared to stand a round he could call it after his home town in Scotland. And so Rutherglen was born. Within months, its population exceeded 20,000. It had 21 hotels, with dancing saloons and other entertainments to cater for men who outnumbered women by 20 to one. The town had its own newspaper, three schools, a police station and a main street lined with shops. A second gold rush in the 1880s led to the discovery of one of Victoria's largest gold reserves. By then, however, grapes rather than gold dominated the economy, with the region producing a quarter of Australia's wine by 1891. Today, Rutherglen is famous as the centre of Australia's oldest wine-growing region.

Having failed to find gold in Australia, lone prospector Louis James Fraser turned to wilder terrain, giving his name to Fraser Hills, Malaysia. Exploring the remote Titiwangsa Mountains of Pahang, he came across not gold but tin deposits, buried in a mossy forest. Opening a mine, he hired Chinese labourers, using mules to transport the ore to town. He branched out, opening gambling and opium dens for off-duty miners. Around 1915 he vanished at the same time as the tin deposits dried up. Two years later, the bishop of Singapore mounted an expedition to find the prospector; he failed to locate Fraser but discovered the region's beauty instead and proposed to the authorities that it would be an ideal site for a hill station. Opened in 1922 as a retreat for

British officials, it soon acquired a golf course and a country club. Today it is one of Malaysia's most popular highland resorts.

Mapping rather than prospecting had led an earlier trekker to the Titiwangsa range, and he too had given his name to a famous mountain resort, the Cameron Highlands. Government surveyor William Cameron, who may have been Scottish, stood on a mountain summit and reported sighting a plateau. He failed, however, to mark the spot on his map and it was only in the 1920s that the site of the plateau was confirmed and earmarked for a hill station.

There is little to connect Orkney, North West Province, South Africa, with the Scottish island other than its name. It recalls the birthplace of Simon Fraser, one of the gold-mining pioneers of the 1880s. The town was proclaimed in 1940 on the farm Witkoppen, where Fraser first started gold mining. The adit that he worked is still used as a ventilation shaft for the modern Orkney mine, which contains some of the richest but deepest gold deposits in South Africa. The town was laid out by another Scot, called Maconachie, who called the streets after British poets and authors.

Mac-Mac Falls, Mpumalanga Province, South Africa, is one of the country's most photographed beauty spots, thanks to the over-enthusiastic Scots. In 1873, the richest strike of gold of its day in South Africa resulted in miners from across the world heading for the area. Hoping for a much easier grasp of the reef containing gold over which a river flowed, they attempted to divert the river by blowing it up with dynamite. The result was spectacular twin waterfalls, which today are a national monument. Thomas François Burgers, President of Transvaal, was invited to visit the goldfields. Burgers proved very popular with the naturally suspicious digger community. He spoke excellent English and his wife, Mary Bryson, was Scots. When the president looked over the claim holders, he noticed the predominance of names prefixed 'Mac' and announced, 'I am going to call this place Mac Mac'; the area became the New Caledonia Goldfields. The ensuing gold rush established the Transvaal Republic as the world's largest gold producer of its day.

'Black gold', namely coal, also played its part in Scottish settlements in South Africa. Halfway between Johannesburg and Durban, Dundee, KwaZulu-Natal was named after an Angus farmer's son, Peter Smith. He bought a farm at Fort Jones, where British soldiers fighting in the Anglo-Zulu War of 1879 had camped. After the soldiers left, Smith started sending wagonloads of coal to be sold in Pietermaritzburg. By 1880, the first proper survey confirmed what locals such as Smith already knew: large, workable coal deposits lay beneath the surface. The Dundee Coal and Estate Company was established and a town planned around the farm to meet the growing need for facilities and housing. The Smith family named the new township Dundee in 1882. It soon emerged as a boom-town, graced with stately homes and the first theatre north of Port Durban. Pioneer traders from the Indian sub-continent settled there after Dundee became the crossroads of seven routes into the African hinterland. Smith floated his coal company on the London Stock Exchange in 1899, the same year as the town witnessed the first shots fired in the Second Boer War. Boer forces occupied Dundee for seven months, renaming it Meyersdorp, but the name Dundee was restored after the British regained the town.

Once nicknamed Coalopolis, Dundee has a population of over 35,000. Two coal mines still operate in the area, one of which is called the Aviemore Mine. Five miles away is the community of Glencoe. The discovery of coal at Dundee demanded a more efficient way to transport it than ox wagons, and so a branch line was built from the Durban–Johannesburg railway in 1903. When the community was incorporated as a town in 1934, it was named Glencoe, a title probably informally given to it by Scottish settlers.

The skills of Scottish miners in extracting 'black gold' transferred easily across the Atlantic. Coal was accidentally discovered at Braidwood, Illinois, when a local farmer was digging a well for water in 1864. The next year Scottish mining engineer James Braidwood, after whom the town was named, sank the first pit, built the first house and fathered Braidwood's first child. As early as 1873 the community was designated a city, having attracted a population of over 2,000. Miners not only from Scotland but from the rest of Britain, Belgium, France, Italy, Germany, Austria, Poland and Bohemia flocked to the area, which was described as 'being nearly akin to Babel of old as regards the confusion of tongues'. By 1873, Braidwood was shipping out 2,000 tons of coal a day and was home to over 1,600 miners.

In the 1870s, Braidwood was a rough-and-ready place, with violence erupting over politics or attempts by the coal owners to reduce wages in times of depression. Brawls were regularly reported in the *Wilmington Advertiser*: 'During a rumpus at Posta's saloon, a beer glass thrown at someone, struck a young son of William Campbell, Sr. cutting fearful gashes in his head and knocking him senseless.' The presence of the miners attracted vagrants and tramps, and women were afraid to leave their homes after dark. Even the local Marshall was shot dead by his friend, a priest who mistook him for an intruder. By the 1880s, seven coal companies operated mines in the area, employing over 2,100 men and benefitting from their closeness to the burgeoning city of Chicago. Mining remained Braidwood's chief occupation until the 1950s; nuclear power is now a major employer within the 6,000-strong community.

Folk singer John Denver immortalised the now vanished coal-mining and iron town of Airdrie Hill, Kentucky, also known as New Airdrie, in his song *Paradise*. The reason why the area was so-called is unknown – possibly because the very first settlers believed they had actually arrived in Paradise. In 1854, a band of miners and iron workers from west central Scotland arrived in the sleepy community to develop the iron ore found about a mile below Paradise. Sir Robert Alexander, a Kentucky-born descendent of a Scottish family, had opened the Airdrie Furnace. He offered to underwrite the fare of any Scotsman willing to emigrate and pay good wages until the works went into operation. A 'new town' sprang up around the works, taking the name of Airdrie after the miners' homeland.

It was a typical boom-or-bust situation. The iron ore proved to be of poor quality and a few months later Alexander moved away, leaving his workers to fend for themselves. Among them was William Graham Duncan, who continued to run the McLean Mine near the furnace. The Duncans later opened mines upriver at Aberdeen and at Graham, which became the largest in West Kentucky. In 1967, the Tennessee Valley Authority, owner of the nearby Paradise Fossil Plant, one of the largest fossil fuel power stations in the USA, moved out the last resident of Airdrie because of ash from the station blowing over the hamlet. Postmaster Buchanan dispatched his last bag of mail. His store, with its huge open fireplace, built to accommodate his tobacco-chewing customers, who could never seem to hit the door of the stove, closed for good.

Full steam ahead

It was at Craigellachie, at the entrance to the Eagle Pass through the Rockies, where Donald Smith hammered in the last spike of the Canadian Pacific Railway (CPR) on 7 November 1885. He had to perform the ceremony twice, as the first spike bent on impact. The settlement took its name from the ancestral war cry of Clan Grant: 'Stand fast, Craigellachie!' This was the message that George Stephen, Donald Smith's cousin and the first chairman of the CPR, had telegraphed to his business associates in Canada when he succeeded in raising desperately needed capital from investors in Britain. The CPR was a remarkable achievement for two young Scots. Donald Smith from Forres is Canada's chief example of a 'rags to riches' story, while George Stephen has been described as 'perhaps the greatest creative genius in the whole history of Canadian finance'.

Inspired by the fur-trading exploits of his maternal uncle, Donald Smith joined the HBC as a clerk in 1838. Rising rapidly through the ranks, he regularly travelled to the company's head-quarters in Montreal, where in 1865 he met his cousin George Stephen, a carpenter's son from Dufftown in Banffshire and by now a wealthy financier. Both men were quick to realise the huge potential of a transcontinental railway, in creating an international trading route from the Far East to Europe, and in carrying emi-grants to farm Canada's empty lands. For Stephen, the CPR was also an investment vehicle; for Smith, it was a means of mod-ernising the HBC's slow and costly transport network. Having turned the bankrupt St Paul and Pacific Railroad, whose route stretched to the Canadian border, into a profitable enterprise, the two men successfully negotiated the contract to build a transcon-tinental railway with the Canadian government in 1880.

The engineering hurdles to be overcome led to the project going well over budget, and the two men had to pledge their homes and their investments to raise the necessary capital to allow the railroad to be completed. An acute shortage of labour also held back progress until, controversially, more than 9,000 Chinese workers were recruited. The Scotsmen's dream was finally realised when the first through-passenger train left Montreal on 28 June 1886, arriving at the Pacific six days later. In 1897, Colonial Secretary Joseph Chamberlain informed Smith that he was to be made a peer. Smith initially chose Lord Glencoe but was prevailed upon to reconsider because of its associations with the massacre. He then created the name Strathcona, a

Gaelic variant on Glencoe. Many Canadian city neighbourhoods adopted the name, from Strathconas in Vancouver, Edmonton and Hamilton to Strathcona Gardens, Burlington; Strathcona Park, Calgary; and Transconas in Winnipeg and Regina.

George Stephen's birthplace was also honoured when naming the railway's Siding 29 Banff. After three railway workers discovered hot springs at Sulphur Mountain, the CPR decided to create a tourist resort, building the first major hotel, the Fairmount Banff Springs, in 1880. When the CPR's general manager, Cornelius Van Horn, paid an inspection visit, he famously remarked: 'Since we can't export the scenery, we'll have to import the tourists.' His eye for detail ensured that the hotel was a success. When, for example, he noticed that guestrooms looked on to trees and the kitchen on to the stunning views of the valley, he reversed the order of the rooms.

Winning national park status encouraged Banff's development. Canadian Prime Minister John Macdonald personally stepped in to resolve conflict between the interests of commercial development and conservation, and to end the dispute as to who had first discovered the hot springs. In 1887, Canada's first national park was created, the Rocky Mountains Park. The resort's first guests were wealthy and adventurous tourists from Europe and North America. Skiing was increasingly popular from the 1920s and by the 1960s Banff was an all-year-round resort.

The railway town of Pitcairn, Pittsburgh, Pennsylvania, has little in common with Banff Springs other than its Scottish title. It was named after Robert Pitcairn, who headed the Pittsburgh Division of the Pennsylvania Railroad in the late nineteenth century. Born in Johnstone, Renfrewshire, Pitcairn's first job was as a messenger boy for the Eastern Telegraph Company, where he worked alongside Andrew Carnegie. When Carnegie left to work for the Pennsylvania Railroad, he got Pitcairn a job as a ticket agent, and when he set up Carnegie Steel, Pitcairn replaced him as head of the railway's Pittsburgh operations. Pitcairn ordered construction of a railyard along Turtle Creek, near Pittsburgh, that was to become the largest in the world.

Sadly, Robert Pitcairn's name was later tarnished through his involvement in one of the largest natural disasters of nineteenth-century America. The exclusive South Fork Fishing and Hunting Club, of which both Carnegie and Pitcairn were members, had altered a dam above Johnstown City to create a fishing lake. Following torrential rain, the dam broke, flooding the city with a 40-foot-high, half-mile-wide wave of water and debris. The death toll rose to 2,209. Although Pitcairn was the first person to alert the Pittsburgh authorities, and he organised blankets and sat on relief committees, he and his fellow club members were blamed for the disaster.

It is unusual to find a Scottish name in the middle of a predom-inantly French map. Robertsonville, Quebec, is the exception, and the railway is the explanation. Founded in 1909 the munici-pality was named after Joseph Gibb Robertson, the president of the Quebec Central Railway. A minister's son from Stuartfield, Aberdeenshire, Joseph emigrated with his family in 1836. The owner of the local flour mill, he actively promoted the railway network and played a part in local and national politics as a Conservative member of the Legislative Assembly of Quebec.

Investing in dreams

William Trent was one of the earliest US businessmen to have a dream – he wanted a country seat and the lifestyle of a gentle-man. He achieved it with Trenton, New Jersey. Little is known of Trent's early life. He may have been born in Inverness around 1650 or have been baptised at South Leith parish church in 1666.

By 1693, he had followed his brother James to Philadelphia, becoming a very wealthy trader in goods and slaves. He owned an interest in 40 ships, exporting tobacco, flour and furs while importing wine, rum, molasses, dry goods and slaves from West Africa and indentured servants from Britain.

In 1714, Trent acquired 800 acres of land in New Jersey, where he built himself a large brick house overlooking the falls of the Delaware River. Seven years later he made it his permanent home. The house was designed in the latest fashion with an avenue of cherry trees leading down to the ferry landing. The estate had various outbuildings and mills along the Assunpink Creek, where in 1720 Trent laid out a new settlement. He was active in local politics, being appointed New Jersey's first resident Chief Justice in 1723. A year later, on Christmas Day, Trent appears to have died suddenly of a stroke.

There is, however, a strange twist to the tale. In 1737, three African slaves were found guilty of murder by poison. It was claimed that one of their victims was William Trent. Trent's country estate grew to become the state capital and for two months in 1784, at the end of the Wars of Independence, the capital of the USA.

Dunfermline-born Andrew Carnegie had a dream to educate future generations through free access to books. It was as a philanthropist rather than as an industrialist that he made his mark on the world map and bought himself immortality. Believing that 'a man who dies rich dies disgraced', he devoted his life and his vast wealth to philanthropy from 1900. He never forgot the influence on his life of Col James Anderson's Mechanics' and Apprentices' Library in Allegheny City. Anderson opened his library of 400 books every Saturday to any poor boy who wanted to borrow a book. After Carnegie, who was working as a messenger boy at the time, wrote to the local newspaper that Anderson's definition of 'poor boys' excluded those who did not work with their hands, Anderson revised his definition to include office workers.

Through his charitable trusts he financed 2,811 Carnegie libraries in America, Canada and the UK. Towns competed to win a free Carnegie library as a means of showing that they had culturally come of age. All they had to do was to put forward a strong case, provide a site and promise to maintain it out of local taxes. Carnegie and East Carnegie, townships within Pittsburgh, Pennsylvania, went as far as to rename their communities so that they would win a Carnegie library. In Australia, the Melbourne suburb of Rosstown changed its name to Carnegie, but this time the tactic was unsuccessful. Carnegie, Oklahoma, had a similar experience. The original name of the small agricultural town was Latham. Shortly after it was incorporated in 1903, community leaders decided to rename it Carnegie in the hope that he would build a library there. Although Carnegie failed to provide the funds, the name was retained: the town's community arts space, the Carnegie Memorial Auditorium, is known as Carnegie Hall.

LEAVING NO TRACE

Wealthy businessmen were drawn to buying islands either as a holiday escape or to put their ideals into practice. In 1918, for example, the soap baron Lord Leverhulme bought the isle of Lewis with the goal of transforming the lives of the Hebridean population by developing the fishing industry. He immortalised his name with his new town of Leverburgh on Harris. On the other side of the globe, Sir Daniel Hamilton left no trace of his name on his social experiment other than the Hamilton Trust through which he bequeathed his assets to the benefit of the islanders of Gosaba, Rangabelia and Satjelia.

In 1903 Arran-born millionaire Sir Daniel Mackinnon Hamilton leased several of the Indian Sundarban islands at the mouth of the Ganges. Hamilton had become one of the richest men in British India through managing the Kolkata-based trading and shipping empire of Mackinnon & Mackenzie. Deeply religious and an admirer of David Livingstone and Adam Smith, Hamilton wanted to use the islands as a social experiment in applying co-operative principles. His motto was 'Labor omnia vincit' (work conquers all).

When Hamilton arrived, the islands were a largely un-inhabited jungle wilderness frequented by tigers and crocodiles. He reclaimed the land using 9,000 day-labourers and encouraged settlers from neighbouring over-populated districts. He built homes in 25 villages, established schools, each with its vegetable plot, co-operative shops, clinics, village councils and co-operative societies. He managed his 10,000 tenants with a firm and principled hand, outlawing money lending and alcohol, and evicting troublemakers. He opened a co-operative rice mill and encouraged villagers to learn new crafts such as weaving. Although Hamilton died in 1939, his islands have found a new role in conserving the tigers which he once encouraged his villagers to shoot as killers.

3

'We're sailing west, we're sailing west . . .'

... To prairie lands, sunkissed and blest
The crofter's trail to happiness.

This emigrant's rhyme, preserved in the Canadian Pacific Railway's Archives, sums up the spirit of Scottish emigration whether to the west or the east.

The history of emigration mirrors the history of modern Scotland, from religious and political persecution to the dramatic impact of the agricultural and industrial revolutions. Resettlement is most closely associated with the Highlands, where population growth meant that crofts were divided again and again. There was simply not enough land to go round. After the Battle of Culloden in 1746, clan chiefs turned into country gentlemen, seeking to capitalise on their landholdings in order to fund their aristocratic lifestyles. The introduction of sheep runs, the failure of the kelp and fishing industries, and potato blight made the situation worse in the 1830s and 1840s when Scotland's population grew by 60 per cent through Irish immigration and natural increase. Land clearance to introduce more efficient farming also took place throughout the rural Lowlands from the late eighteenth century.

The first wave of emigration included those tenant farmers with the foresight to see that they would soon be moved from the land. Some landowners such as the Dukes of Argyll and Sutherland encouraged tenants to emigrate by offering financial incentives: others simply evicted their crofting tenants. The Emigration Act of 1851 made the option of starting a new life more freely available to the poorest people: for example, landlords could secure a passage to Australia for nominated tenants at the cost of £1, with the Highlands and Islands Emigration Society overseeing the process of resettlement.

Although escaping grinding poverty and the toil of eking a subsistence living from an inhospitable land was the driver for many emigrants, there was also the pull of making a new life in a young country. The chance of adventure and wealth had strong appeal, especially to single, young men. These pioneers wrote home inviting their relatives to join them in a 'land of milk and honey', their descriptions of which often bore little resemblance to the struggle to tame the forested wilderness. The authorities in Canada and Australia – whose challenge was the opposite of Scotland's – could boast mile upon mile of empty land but not enough people to farm it, and they actively promoted emigration. Ironically, the settlers often took over land which had been cleared of native people to make way for the newcomers.

Canada was the first choice for many, as it allowed them to put down roots in a land similar to home. The first major group were former soldiers who had fought with the British in the American Wars of Independence. Landlords funded whole communities to emigrate, and the great trading companies sought Scottish seafaring expertise and ability to withstand harsh conditions. Nearly 60 per cent of UK emigrants to Nova Scotia, for example, were born in Scotland. As Canada opened up, many settlers headed further west in the late nineteenth century, encouraged by offers of free or cheap land from provincial governments, the railroads and companies set up for the purpose, such as the Commercial Colonisation Company of Manitoba.

The first Scottish settlers in Australia had little choice in the matter. They made up a significant proportion of the 165,000 people in Britain sentenced to transportation by the courts from 1788 to 1856. Some ex-convicts chose to stay on at the end of their sentence to be joined by settlers from throughout the predominantly rural areas of Scotland. Australia was hungry for people and talent. From the 1830s, assisted emigration schemes and opportunities in sheep farming provided additional incentives to both the adventurous and the destitute. New Zealand was another popular destination, with Scots making up a quarter of the population by 1850.

From the late nineteenth century until it closed its doors to immigrants in the late 1920s, the USA became the chosen destination for over half of emigrating Scots, its large-scale building projects, its industries and fast-growing cities offering opportunities for those with skills in everything from blacksmithing to mining.

Although the number of emigrants was never as large as for Canada, Australia and New Zealand, South Africa was increasingly popular with the middle classes and skilled workers: in the inter-war period, 21,000 people headed for South Africa compared with nearly 200,000 whose destination was Canada.

In the nineteenth century, Scotland was second only to Ireland and Norway in the scale of emigration, and exceeded them both in the run-up to and immediately after the First World War, when those leaving made up a fifth of the working population. Thereafter, as economic depression and war spread across the globe, many countries closed their doors to immigrants. In the 1950s, assisted passage schemes attracted skilled workers and professionals to Canada, New Zealand and Australia, with its influx of 'ten pound Poms'.

Emigrants took their personal belongings and a few treasured possessions like a favourite ornament, the family Bible or a sheepdog across the oceans. Some even shipped wheels and axles, made by a trusted local craftsman, as the base for transport in the backwoods. For most, it was a one-way trip. Their legacy was to leave the name of the place which they had previously called home. Abernethy, Ben Lomond, Cupar, Douglas . . . to list every settlement, especially in parts of Canada, the USA, Australia and New Zealand, would fill a volume and many of the reasons for the choice of name are identical. This selection has been made to reflect both the typical and the unusual.

First find your land and then farm it

The distinction between explorer and emigrant is often a fine one. Allan Cunningham, whose father came from Renfrewshire, discovered and named the Macintyre River, which runs along the border between Queensland and New South Wales, in 1827. This was his seventh expedition as a botanical collector for the Royal Gardens at Kew. He travelled north from the Hunter Valley to discover the Darling Downs. He called the river after Peter MacIntyre, whose family had provided him with horses and guides.

Born in Tomcairn, Perthshire, MacIntyre was the land agent of politician and coloniser Thomas MacQueen, who had devised a plan whereby settlers with sufficient capital to employ convicts would be granted land to settle New South Wales. Macintyre arrived in Sydney in 1825, his two ships carrying the first free emigrants to Australia – shepherds, mechanics and farmers. Macintyre selected the land, naming the acreage that he had secured for himself Blairmore; that assigned to MacQueen was named Segenhoe. In 1838, MacQueen laid out a new town, calling it Aberdeen after his friend and fellow politician George Hamilton Gordon, the 4th Earl of Aberdeen. Although he ended up bankrupt, his new town flourished with the establishment of Australia's first horse-drawn flour mill and an inn by 1840. Later the small town in the Hunter Valley became an important food industry centre, the Aberdeen Butter Factory marketing Thistle Butter.

Macintyre aimed to be first to occupy the land around the river which bore his name, having heard from his friend Allan Cunningham about its 'beautiful sward of grass'. He dispatched one of his five overseers, Alexander Campbell, to stake out a cattle station for him at Byron Plains. As well as administering Macintyre's Hunter Valley property at Blairmore, Argyllshire-born Campbell, who had emigrated in 1825, seized a slice of the action for himself. He established his own sheep-run station next door to Byron Plains, which he called Inverell. The name came from the Gaelic *inver* – the Macintyre River ran through his property – and *ell*, meaning a swan. At its peak in the late nineteenth century, Inverell station boasted 100,000 sheep, 4,000 head of cattle and up to 200 pure-bred Clydesdale horses. The town later earned its nickname of 'Sapphire City' as it produced four-fifths of the world's sapphires, as well as being a leading supplier of Zircon, industrial diamonds and tin.

Another unrelated member of the Campbell clan also settled in the Hunter Valley. John Campbell named his land, granted in 1826, Cessnock after his grandfather's castle near Kilmarnock to stress his aristocratic associations. The city of Cessnock was built on the site of his farm, although it remained a rural backwater until the discovery of coal in 1892. The city has an unusual claim to fame: its swimming pool, built in 1934, was not only Australia's first created to Olympic standards but the first in the world to use black tiles as lane markers. It has honoured its Campbell founder with a statue.

The story of Scone, New South Wales, starts with Allan Cunningham and a Scottish convict ship's doctor, William Bell Carlyle. He made his third trip in 1824 on the *Henry*, whose passengers included 69 female convicts and 25 free women who were joining their convict husbands. This was the year that Cunningham's surveyors and botanists were exploring the upper Hunter Valley. Carlyle recommended taking out a land grant to his Ecclefechan-born nephews, Francis and Archibald Little, who became among the earliest European settlers in the Hunter Valley. The three men farmed adjacent properties: Carlyle at Satur, where a landmark is still called Carlyle's Gully; Francis at Invermein and Archibald at Cressfield, both named after family properties around Ecclefechan. Carlyle has also the dubious distinction of introducing the prickly pear to Australia, a leaf of which he had brought from India to adorn Mrs Francis Little's garden. It took a century to eradicate the rapidly spreading plant.

The Invermein homestead soon attracted a settlement, with a lock-up, a Court of Petty Sessions and a post office. In 1831, Hugh Cameron, an elderly Scottish settler, petitioned the governor to name the valley Strathearn after its Scottish counterpart close to the Palace of Scone, the ancient crowning place of the kings of Scotland. Strathearn became the parish of the area and Invermein village settlement graduated to Scone town, laid out in 1837. Scone's commercial status was confirmed in the 1870s with the arrival of the railway, a public school, a bank and the creation of a Catholic Parish. In 1957, Scone Municipality amalgamated with Upper Hunter Shire to become Scone Shire.

Today, Scone is known as a horse breeding centre, sometimes being referred to as 'the Horse Capital of Australia', and for the Birnam Wood winery at Dunsinane.

Braidwood, New South Wales, is named after Thomas Wilson, explorer, eminent Sydney surgeon, landowner and Scot, whose middle name was Braidwood. Born in Uphall, West Lothian, Wilson became a naval surgeon in 1815. He served on several convict ships headed for New South Wales and Tasmania, treating the convicts with a degree of humanity, and reducing the death rate by insisting on cleanliness and a daily issue of lime juice and wine. He taught them how to read and write, conducted divine service and would not permit 'the slightest slang, flash songs nor swearing' to ward against further personal degradation. On these voyages he took the opportunity to explore: Wilson's Inlet in King George Sound is named after him. On another voyage in 1831, he introduced many European plants and the first hive of bees to survive in Australia.

In 1822, Wilson bought land on the Macquarie River in Tasmania, which he named Janefield after his wife. Four years later he was allowed to transfer this grant to New South Wales, where he was also given 5,000 acres as a reward for his explorations in 'the western part of New Holland'. He called part of his land Braidwood. When the site for a new town centre was chosen in 1833, it fell on part of Wilson's property and the town took its name from his Braidwood Estate. Back in Britain in 1835, he published *Narrative of a Voyage Round the World*, giving an account of his adventures. In the appendix, he commented on the treatment of prisoners in convict transports and praised Australia as a place for intending emigrants. The next year he brought his wife, daughter and son to Braidwood. He was respected as an efficient farmer and magistrate, although he was declared bankrupt in 1843 and died a month later.

When gold was discovered in the 1850s, Braidwood was transformed, although crime arrived with prosperity. So extreme was the extent of lawlessness that in 1867 the government ordered a Royal Commission to investigate. Thereafter, with gold mining in decline and bypassed by the railway, Braidwood shrank. Rediscovered in the late 1970s, its boom-town architecture was restored and in 2006 it became the first complete town to be placed on the New South Wales State Heritage Register.

The Archer family from Perth were among the earliest settlers in Queensland. David, the first brother to arrive in 1834, worked in his cousin's Sydney wool-exporting business and, incidentally, failed to introduce Charles Darwin to a kangaroo! Later joined by William, Thomas, Charles and John, the brothers set up sheep runs and started to reconnoitre virgin territory for its grazing potential. It was on one of these forays that Charles and William discovered the Fitzroy River, Queensland, the second-largest river catchment in Australia, in 1853. They named it in honour of Sir Charles Fitzroy, governor of New South Wales. In the same year, Thomas returned home to marry Grace Morrison; the family partnership called one of their sheep runs Gracemere in her honour. The city of Rockhampton now stands on part of the Gracemere land.

Place names in Gippsland, Victoria, recall the exploits of one of the many Scottish explorers-turned-pastoralists so typical of the early days of European settlement in Australia. Except for a twist of fate, Gippsland might have been named Caledonia Australis. Born in Glenbrittle on Skye, Angus McMillan arrived in New South Wales from Greenock in 1838. Deeply religious, he was disgusted by the treatment of convict labour and moved inland, where he befriended and learned bushcraft from the local Aborigines. Climbing Mount McLeod, he caught his first glimpse of the plains and lakes of what became Gippsland. The next year he set off with a party of fellow pioneers, convicts and Aborigines to explore the potential of the area which he called Caledonia Australis. In 1840, a rival explorer, Pavel Strzelecki, followed the tracks first made by McMillan and gave his own titles to the landscape features that he passed. Although McMillan's names were officially adopted for rivers such as the Caledonia, the Aberfeldy and the Macalister, Gippsland, honouring the governor of New South Wales, Sir George Gipps, won out over Caledonia Australis.

His travelling days over, McMillan settled at Bushy Park, where he farmed, entertained, raced horses against his neighbours and fulfilled the duties of president of the Gippsland Caledonian Society. His home became a haven for newly arrived Scots. In 1864, he took off on his travels again, having been appointed leader of the government's Alpine expedition to open tracks in mining areas. Most of his party abandoned him when they discovered the Pioneer gold deposit. Alone, he pursued his last trail towards the future Bairnsdale but died en route after one of his packhorses stumbled and rolled on top of him. One of the settlers whom McMillan hoped to encourage was a fellow emigrant from Skye, Captain Norman McLeod. He named his sheep station after his home village Bernisdale. A township grew up and hijacked the name to reflect the fact that local children liked to play in the surrounding dales.

New Zealand's first settlers

William and John Deans were the first permanent European residents of New Zealand's Canterbury Plains, the only previous settler having been driven away by rats. Their legacy was Riccarton, Christchurch. The brothers had been baptised in Riccarton, Ayrshire, in the late 1810s. After training as lawyers, they were tempted by the New Zealand Company's colonising scheme. They were assigned the right to farm at Puturingamotu provided that they did not settle near Maori plantings. In 1843, William Deans set sail from Wellington with two other Scottish families, the Gebbies and the Mansons. The party took a whale-boat up the river, which Deans later named Avon after the stream in Lanarkshire close to where his grandfather lived. They then switched to a canoe that could cope with shallow water. They built the first European house on the Canterbury Plains, held together with wooden pegs, as they had accidentally left the nails in Wellington. The house was divided into three compartments to house the three families until in 1845 the Mansons and the Gebbies were ready to establish their own farms at the head of the harbour.

In 1848, the brothers signed an agreement with the New Zealand Company, who had bought land for what became the settlement of Christchurch. The Deans brothers were allowed to keep 400 acres for their farm at Riccarton. As a result of limitations on their landholdings, the brothers decided to move their stock to a sheep run of 15,000 acres in what they called the Morven Hills. In 1851, on an expedition to Australia to purchase more sheep, William drowned when his ship was wrecked. John returned to Scotland the following year to marry Jane McIlraith, who had waited ten long years for him to wed and bring her to New Zealand. Sadly, their time together was short. John developed tuberculosis, his last wish being that Riccarton Bush remained wild land forever. His wish was honoured as, on Jane's death in 1911, the Deans family presented Riccarton Bush to the people of Canterbury.

From 1846, Scots emigrants started to settle the area around Otago in New Zealand's South Island. They named the river Clutha after the Gaelic name for the Clyde. It was a significant naming, as the Clutha is the second-longest river in New Zealand, and the swiftest and highest by volume of water. James McNeil from Bonhill in Dunbartonshire is regarded as the founder of the town of Balclutha, as he established a ferry at the river mouth in 1857. The settlement grew rapidly during the Otago gold rush, changing its name from Clutha Ferry to Balclutha, 'the town on the Clyde'.

Recruiting settlers to the USA

As well as the millions of Scots who found their own passage to a new life, land promoters actively sought out Scottish recruits. Happily, the town of Darien, Georgia, had better prospects than that of the disastrous Darien Scheme in Panama. General James Edward Oglethorpe founded the colony of Georgia at Savannah in 1733. Realising the need for military outposts to protect the new settlement against Native Americans, he dispatched Hugh Mackay and George Dunbar to Scotland to seek recruits. A band of 177 Highlanders, mainly members of the Clan Chattan from around Inverness, arrived on the *Prince of Wales* at Savannah, where Oglethorpe ordered them to start planning a settlement at the mouth of the Altamaha River.

Led by John Mohr Mackintosh and Hugh Mackay, the group set up cannons on the earthworks of Fort St George, built huts and erected a small church where the Reverend John McLeod from Skye preached weekly. Despite being an Englishman, Oglethorpe held his first military review in 1736 dressed in full Highland regalia. Later that year he returned to lay out the new town on a bluff overlooking the river about a mile west of the fort. The settlers called it Darien, in memory of the Darien venture in Panama. Captain Dunbar reported: 'The Scots desire their town shall be called Darien.' Initially, the town itself was called New Inverness to separate it from the recently established District of Darien.

In 1818, Darien became the seat of county government. By the 1830s, it had reached the height of its commercial prosperity, with the Bank of Darien prospering from its backing of gold fields and the port booming with exports of timber and cotton. The port later declined after the timber upstream was exhausted and Darien was bypassed by the railroads. In the late nineteenth century oyster fishing came to the rescue, but it too was exhausted by over-harvesting. Along with tourism, fishing for the famous Wild Georgia Shrimp and blue crab are now mainstays of the economy.

> I like the climate and the soil, I like the people, too;
> I like the sagebrush desert and I like the mountain view
> Of all the towns I've ever seen, the one that suits me best
> Is the little town of Aberdeen, in Idaho, out west.

> – Jap Toner, first publisher of the *Aberdeen Times*

A few gold prospectors, cattlemen and pioneer farmers first moved into the 'arid lands' of the Snake River Valley around Aberdeen, Idaho, in the 1860s. The passing of the Desert Land Act (the Carey Act) of 1894 quickened the pace of development. The Act sought to release millions of acres in the western states that required irrigation for productive farming. Individual states were empowered to initiate reclamation projects, selling the land at a nominal price in return for the longer term benefits of increased tax revenue. Development companies proposed, designed and built suitable irrigation projects, making their profits by selling water to the settlers. Idaho was a particular beneficiary of the Act, with up to 60 per cent of all US acreage irrigated by Carey Act projects being in the state.

Idaho's first Carey Act initiative was the Aberdeen-Springfield Canal Company. Work on the canal began in 1901 to deliver water to potential farmland and irrigate the crop for which Aberdeen became famous: potatoes. The company divided its land into residential, commercial, farm and industrial lots that were sold to individuals through a lottery. A $50 lottery ticket guaranteed a one-way fare to Aberdeen on the Oregon Short-line Railroad and a plot in the town of Aberdeen. In 1909, a Mr Sweet was manager of the company that had recently acquired the Aberdeen coal mine and helped to refinance the canal company. He recalled the reason for selecting the name: 'Partly in their honor [the directors were from Scotland or of Scotch descent] and partly because we all liked the name, we called the town Aberdeen.' Another theory is that choosing a name starting with 'Ab' ensured a prominent place at the start of telephone and business directories.

Scotsman John Hamilton Gillespie turned a small community into the city of Sarasota, Florida. There had been flirtations with the infant orange-growing business, but the district only started to take off when the Edinburgh-based Florida Investment and Mortgage Company bought 60,000 acres of land. In 1885, with the lure of settling in 'a sunny paradise', it dispatched 65 Scots to the area. An unusually cold winter and a much harder life than had been promised forced all but three families and a few individuals to leave. The Mortgage Company had been misled – Sarasota consisted of one building and a trail.

To keep their colonial venture from turning into a disaster, the directors of Florida Mortgage appointed John Gillespie, the chairman's son, as a trouble shooter. Arriving in 1886, he re-cruited work crews to lay out the new town and within months he had built a house for himself. A newspaper, a rail link and a telephone line quickly followed. As well as encouraging the fishing industry, Gillespie established a steamship link with Tampa and a hotel for winter tourists. Gradually, the future city took shape, being incorporated in 1902 with John Gillespie as the first mayor, a position he held for six consecutive terms.

No one knows the origin of the name Sarasota or why it was chosen. Some people suggest that it relates to Sara, reputedly the daughter of conquistador DeSota. Others link it to the Native American word *sara-se-cota*, meaning a landfall easily observed from the sea. At the time of Gillespie's arrival, the tiny community was called Osprey and a nearby settlement Fruitville.

Gillespie was passionate about golf and had packed his hickory sticks to take with him to Florida. He laid out a two-hole 'course' behind his house in 1886 which by 1901 had acquired nine holes and a clubhouse. Gillespie's 'course' lies behind Sarasota's claim as 'the Cradle of Golf in the USA', while Robert Lockhart from Dunfermline, who set up the first golf club – St Andrews, Yonkers – with a membership of seven in 1887, is also claimed as 'the Father of US golf'. Appropriately Gillespie died on the golf course. In 1910, he had sold his land interests to Owen Burns, whose ancestors emigrated from Ayrshire in 1734. Burns, who is commemorated in Burns Square, continued the city's development. Today, with a population of over 50,000, Sarasota is twinned with Dunfermline in Fife and 'the Scot who saved Sarasoto' is honoured in its annual festival, which has a distinctly tartan twist.

Old problems, new opportunities

The wide open spaces of Canada presented the opportunity to solve problems at home. At the close of the War of 1812, the British government was faced with two challenges: unemployment and depression at home, and an uneasy peace with the

Surviving Scottish place names on Prince Edward Island

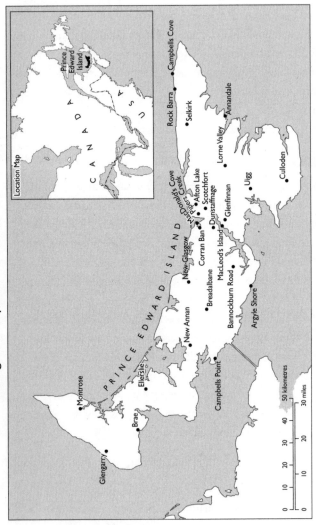

Given that Prince Edward Island is described as 'the most Scottish province of Canada', it is not surprising that the legacy of Scottish place names is strong both for settlements and features in the landscape. Many early nineteenth-century emigrants came from the West Highlands and islands, choosing names that reflected their nostalgia for the homeland. Others opted to commemorate ancient battles or the 1745 Jacobite rebellion, which, for a few, would still be within living memory. Although some places are farming communities or coastal hamlets, their inhabitants are still proud of their Scottish roots.

Americans abroad. Its policy was to settle the interior of Ontario as a second line of defence against further hostilities, as well as an outlet for unemployed tradesmen and discharged soldiers. An emigration scheme was put in place to settle the great wilderness north and west of the Rideau River. Perth was established as a British military settlement and by autumn 1816, 1,500 people had moved into the area, including many Scottish ex-soldiers and stonemasons.

The military regime lasted until 1824, when the land was laid out into counties and townships, usually taking the names of places in the old country, like Perth itself. The construction of the Rideau Canal and the development of the lumber trade led to Perth being overshadowed by 'Bytown', the future city of Ottawa.

Perth has several other Scottish claims to fame: the last fatal duel in Canada took place here in 1833 between two love-lorn emigrants from Inverurie and Paisley who had quarrelled over the local school teacher; and dentist Dr J. F. Kennedy installed the first Bell telephone between his home and his office in the town. By 1887, there were 19 telephones in Perth, with its switch-board being in the office of Dr Kennedy, who was a friend of the inventor of the telephone, Alexander Graham Bell. The Tay Canal, which links Perth to the Rideau Canal, winds up the Tay River, through the Tay Marsh and into the Tay River Basin. In 2000, Perth, Ontario, became the twin town of Perth, Scotland.

Perth is one of eight municipalities that make up Lanark County. Three others have Scottish names – Tay Valley, Lanark Highlands and Drummond North. Located on the Clyde River, the town of New Lanark dropped the 'New' over time. It too was originally a government supply depot and military base. By spring 1821, 1,500 people had settled around Lanark, the

majority of whom were unemployed Scottish weavers and discharged soldiers. That summer a further 1,800 Scottish emigrants
arrived.

Galloway landowner Thomas Douglas, 5th Earl of Selkirk,
was one of the most famous promoters of emigration schemes.
He was so shocked by the harsh treatment of crofters cleared
from their lands in the Highlands that he decided to use his
inheritance to back emigrant settlements in Canada. Motivated
by both philanthropy and ambition, he envisaged the creation of a
model Scottish village for Highlanders facing overpopulation and
scarce resources. In 1803, he escorted 800 emigrants, many of
whom were from Skye, Raasay, North Uist and Mull, to Belfast,
Prince Edward Island. They arrived after a journey which could
take three months in rough weather. By the time the last settlers
landed, the first group had erected a temporary encampment of
wigwams. Within a year, they were self-sufficient farmers.

The Selkirk settlers were not the first Scots to step foot on
Prince Edward Island. Captain John MacDonald of Glenalladale
had brought over several hundred Roman Catholic Highlanders
between 1770 and 1775. They settled around Tracadie Bay,
where they planted the island's first potatoes. Several hundred
Protestant Scottish Lowlanders settled around Malpeque Bay.
By the mid-1800s Scots represented over half of the island's
population, making Prince Edward Island the most 'Scottish'
province or state in North America. Names on rural mailboxes
still recall these adventurous emigrants: MacRae, MacLeod,
MacDonald, MacLean, MacPherson, Beaton, Cameron, Gillis,
Morrison, Murchison and Ross. Places on the map include
Annandale, Breadalbane, Inverness, Montrose, New Glasgow
and St Andrews Parish, while landscape features include the rivers Clyde, Glenfinnan and Murray, the last named after the East
Lothian-born Governor of Quebec.

Later in 1803, the Earl of Selkirk purchased land at Baldoon, Ontario, for a second settlement, naming it after Baldoon in Wigtownshire. Around 100 members of 15 families, mainly recruited from Mull, arrived the next year. They had agreed to work on Selkirk's estate for several years in return for a free passage. The settlement soon hit problems from which it never recovered. The marshes, which regularly flooded, proved difficult to farm and were a breeding ground for mosquitoes. The estate manager, Alexander McDonnell, was regularly absent, pursuing other interests. But by 1806 things had started to look up and one settler wrote home urging his brother to join him: 'There is not a place under the sun better than this place.' During the War of 1812, US troops raided the village, destroying homes and stealing livestock. Selkirk sold the farm and the name died with it. It was renamed Wallaceburg, in honour of the Scottish fighter, and the settlement around it thrived in the long term, building its economy from timber and boatbuilding.

Now suburbs of Winnipeg, Point Douglas and Kildonan are reminders of the earl's last venture, the Red River Settlement. By 1811, the earl and his relatives had infiltrated the Hudson's Bay Company and persuaded it to let him settle the area around the Winnipeg basin on condition that emigrants did not enter the fur trade. He also acquired a smaller piece of land at Pembina, North Dakota. In one of the earliest and most infamous clearances, in 1812 the future Duke of Sutherland's factors removed nearly 2,000 people from the fertile Strath of Kildonan near Helmsdale to make way for sheep. Many younger crofters opted for the Red River Settlement. The first emigrants from Kildonan set sail on the HBC's ship, the *Prince of Wales*, in 1813. A second contingent of more than 700 crofters joined them two years later.

Their initial experience was fraught. The first settlers arrived in the midst of a fierce struggle between the HBC and its rival fur-trading empire, the NWC, for control of the vast territory. Frost, gales and grasshoppers attacked their crops. The first governor of the settlement, Alexander McDonell from Inverness-shire, was eventually dismissed for dishonesty, drunkenness and causing dissension among the settlers. The settlement was slow to grow and only in 1855 did William Scott become the first postmaster in Western Canada.

McNab, Renfrew County, Ontario, was one of Canada's strangest social experiments. Born in Glendochart, Perthshire, Archibald, the 'Last Laird of the Clan MacNab', fled to Canada in 1822 to escape his creditors. His vision was to transplant the clan system lock, stock and barrel to a Canadian setting. Having acquired land near Ottowa, he summoned 100 clansmen from Scotland in 1825. When Scottish engineer John MacTaggart visited the settlement a few years later, he wrote: 'this is a beautiful place! Here stands the Castle of Mac Nab, surrounded by the houses of his followers.' All was not well, however, as MacNab ruled his community with an iron fist, treating the settlers like slaves. They rebelled, although it took 18 years of 'peaceful resistance' – petitions, court battles and legal manoeuvres – before they succeeded in ousting their chief.

The Buchanans were one of the families who came over in 1825. Six years later they built a small sawmill and bridge on the Madawaska River, naming the new settlement after Arnprior in Stirlingshire. In 1851, Daniel McLachlin, the Canadian-born son of a Highland Scot, recognised the potential of Arnprior as a logging operation. By the turn of the twentieth century, Arnprior boasted the largest white pine sawmill in North America. Today the small town of just over 7,000 people is a centre for agriculture, tourism and hydroelectric-power generation.

Investing in Canada

The ceremonial felling of a maple tree marked the foundation of Guelph, Ontario, on St George's Day, 1827. The man with the vision behind the new settlement, one of the first planned towns in Canada, was Scottish novelist and developer John Galt. As a storyteller, Galt appreciated that the swing of the axe provided a suitably dramatic birth for his new town. He recorded in his autobiography how 'the tree fell with a crash of accumulating thunder. After a funereal pause, the doctor pulled a flask of whiskey from his bosom, and we drank prosperity to the City of Guelph.' The doctor was William 'Tiger' Dunlop from Greenock, adventurer, soldier, writer and Galt's right-hand man.

The Canada Company, which financed the new town, was Galt's brainchild. He raised £1 million from British businessmen to buy large amounts of land acquired by the Crown from First Nation people. The company made its profits by selling lots to an anticipated flood of European settlers. Galt's deal for 1.3 million acres of Upper Canada's remaining unleased Crown reserves included the 42,000-acre Halton Block that became Guelph and the one-million-acre Huron Tract, where he founded the town of Goderich. Galt chose the name Guelph to honour George IV, whose Hanoverian Guelph family lineage stretched back for over a thousand years. His choice of name ruffled feathers back home, being seen as a slight to Lord Goderich, who had assisted in the formation of the Canada Company. Galt solved the problem by naming his second settlement Goderich.

Galt laid out Guelph like a European city. A series of five boulevards fanned out from a central point on the Speed River, with squares and narrower streets in between. On the ground, development was more modest, Guelph's first building serving as temporary lodging for settlers, a tavern, a post office, a school and Galt's own home. By late 1827, 70 homes had been built, including the Priory, the nascent city's most important public building, which could accommodate a hundred newcomers, as well as housing the company offices and a tavern. Among the first settlers was a party of 135 Clearance Highlanders whose earlier attempt at emigration had ended in disaster. When the land in La Guaira, Venezuela, proved impossible to cultivate, they were advised to move to Canada. An official at the British Consulate in New York, who was a friend of Galt's, suggested that they make for Guelph.

Galt's experiment ended badly. His haphazard book-keeping and reluctance to consult his backers resulted in his being summoned home in 1829. Although he participated in one last land scheme, the Eastern Townships of Lower Canada, he never returned to his adopted country. The Canada Company proved a more ruthless landlord and the settlers were too poor to support many shops or hotels. Despite Galt's grandiose plans, Guelph had to wait for the arrival of the railway in 1856 to become more than a village. Population growth was fuelled not by Scots emigrants but by freed black slaves.

Galt's felling of the maple tree is remembered in the city's coat of arms, where an axeman stands proud as the left supporter. The city is still known as 'the Royal City' because it was the first place in the world to adopt this particular royal association.

Although he did not adopt Scottish names for his settlements, Galt himself is still remembered in the Galt district of Cambridge, Ontario. Until government reorganisation in 1973, Galt was a separate town, tracing its roots back to 1791, when the First Nation people sold some of their reserve lands along the Grand River for development. One land purchaser was Dumfries-born lawyer William Dickson, who had money to invest. He divided his land, which became known as North and South Dumfries, into smaller plots to market to Scots would-be settlers through a recruitment agent in Scotland backed by advertisements in the Scottish press. By 1832, every plot was filled.

Dickson chose a site at the confluence of Mill Creek and the Grand River for his main township, known locally as Shade's Mills. When it was large enough to warrant a post office, Dickson chose Galt, in honour of the Scottish novelist and Commissioner of the Canada Company. The settlers were slow to change, preferring the more familiar Shade's Mills until John Galt visited in person in 1827. Galt rapidly grew into an industrial centre, earning it the nickname 'the Manchester of Canada'.

Galt has another Scottish connection – Blair Atholl. Born among the Campsie Hills, Dunbartonshire, in 1833, evangelical missionary Annie Macpherson was distressed by the plight of orphans and other destitute children in British workhouses. She organised a programme to support their emigration to Canada to live with and work for farmers who were desperately short of labour. In 1872, she established Blair Atholl, a 100-acre farm in Galt, where newly arrived children could learn basic skills before being placed on a farm, equipped with a year's supply of clothes, writing materials and a Bible. She chose the name Blair Atholl as it was a place she had liked from childhood days. The home moved to Stratford, Ontario, in 1882, one report suggesting that the residents of Galt were becoming weary of fundraising appeals.

Named for a fraud

A few place names have come about through fraud. New Orleans, Louisiana, was the brainchild of John Law, who came from a Fife banking family. Born in 1761, he was brought up in

Lauriston Castle, then a country estate outside Edinburgh. He believed that money was a means of exchange rather than of wealth per se and that national prosperity depended on trade. A brilliant economist and gambler, Law charmed his way through European financial capitals until he caught the attention of the Duc d'Orléans, regent of a bankrupt France after the death of Louis XIV. The Duc readily accepted Law's plan, later known as the Mississippi Bubble, to establish a private bank, the Royal Bank of France, using paper currency with the riches of the part of Louisiana that the French still owned to be used as collateral. Law's venture depended on the successful establishment of a colony able to pay interest on company shares. He named the capital of his colony New Orleans after the Duc, even before a site for it had been identified in 1718, and recruited French settlers, who did not take kindly to the harsh living conditions. Law had to look further afield, to Germany and Switzerland, to find people tempted by 'a land filled with gold, silver, copper, and lead mines'. Many did not survive the journey on the 'pest ships'. Speculation on the worth of the colony caused shares to sky-rocket before plummeting. Law was forced to flee and spent his last years back at the gambling tables of Europe.

The Principality of Poyais, Honduras, must be the strangest Scottish emigration scheme of all. Gregor MacGregor, the self-styled Serene Highness Gregor I of Poyais, was one of the biggest fraudsters in British history. Born in 1786 close to the shores of Loch Katrine in Stirlingshire, MacGregor made a career as a soldier of fortune. He was created a General by the South American independence leader Simón Bolívar and married his niece, Josefa. Although cashiered by the British Army, MacGregor was feted in London society when he arrived in 1821, claiming to be the Prince of Poyais, ruler of an area larger than Wales.

MacGregor produced a 350-page guidebook, supposedly written by a Captain Thomas Strangeways, extolling the beauty of Poyais, with its friendly natives, mild climate, streams filled with gold, abundant forests and European-style capital. He persuaded hundreds of emigrants to buy land and floated a fabricated government loan on the London stock exchange, which attracted hundreds of gullible investors. He established offices for the 'Legation of the Territory of Poyais' in Edinburgh and Glasgow, claiming that his promised land would appeal to hardy and adventurous Highlanders, as they would have the right skills and character.

In 1823, an advance party of more than 200 Scots and their families set off in two ships from Leith and London. In all, MacGregor had recruited seven shiploads, but the navy turned back the other five when news of the reality of Poyais started to leak out. When the settlers arrived at the aptly named Mosquito Coast on the Bay of Honduras, they found a swamp hemmed in by jungle and the ruins of a previous settlement. That spring 200 settlers died, one being eaten by an alligator and one shooting himself on discovering that he was not to become the royal shoemaker. Eventually a ship rescued them and took them to nearby Belize. Of the 320 people who joined the fraudulent scheme only 50 returned to Britain, a few staying on in Belize or emigrating to America. Although there was a public inquiry in Belize into the fraud, MacGregor was exonerated. He then tried to pull off the same scam in France but was rumbled and asked to leave. A con-artist to the end, MacGregor persuaded the Venezuelan government to grant him a pension because of his military service and was buried in Caracas in 1845 with full military honours. Despite raising the equivalent of £3.6 billion in scams over his lifetime, his name appears today on a monument to the heroes of Venezuelan independence in Caracas.

THE CAMPBELLS ARE COMING

The world atlas lists over 40 settlements and landscape features that include the word Campbell. This selection illustrates some of the ways in which the Campbells acquired their names:

- Campbell, New York State, was named after settler Robert Campbell, who emigrated from Glasgow in the 1790s.

- Campbell, Nebraska, honoured the Superintendent of the Burlington & Missouri Railroad, who emigrated to Canada as a child in 1848. The railroad promoted the development of towns on its land.

- Campbellsville, Kentucky, was named by Andrew Campbell and his brothers, who laid out the settlement in 1817. Moving here from Virginia, they were probably originally Ulster-Scots.

- Cape Campbell, New Zealand, was named by Captain Cook in 1770 when sailing round the South Island. He may have chosen to honour John Campbell, the naval officer and navigational expert born in Kirkbean outside Dumfries in 1720.

- Campbellfield, Victoria, Australia, was named after one of the two Campbells who first farmed the area. The Scots church dates back to 1842.

- Campbellford, Ontario, takes its name from two Scots-born brothers, Lieutenant-Colonel Robert Campbell and Major David Campbell, who took up the British government's offer of land to retiring officers in 1831.

- Campbell Creek, Alaska, was named by explorer Captain George Vancouver or a member of his crew in 1794. The Campbell in question was Elizabeth, daughter of the 2nd Duke of Argyll and wife of the Scottish politician and astronomer John Stuart MacKenzie. He is commemorated in the neighbouring MacKenzie Creek.

- Campbellpur, India, was founded in 1908 and named after the military hero Sir Colin Campbell. Since 1978 the city has reverted to its Indian name, Attock.

- While there are at least eight Campbelltowns or Campbelltons around the world, there is only one Campbeltown and it is in Scotland.

4

Up country

Kentucky's wood-encumbered brake,
Or wild Ontario's boundless lake.

- Sir Walter Scott, Marmion

As Scots headed west, they might pack their favourite author, whether Scott, Burns or the Bible, on their wagons alongside their household chattels and farm implements. Some emigrants moved several times over the generations. Their initial choice may have proved disappointing, having been oversold by emigration-scheme promoters and shipping agents. As the young countries grew and hinterlands were opened up, new opportunities presented themselves backed by available finance from colonial governments, railway companies and private investors. The Aberdeen-based North of Scotland Canadian Mortgage Company, for example, moved its Canadian headquarters from Toronto to Winnipeg to reflect the volume of business from the prairie provinces. Some emigrants may simply have been born with a spirit of wanderlust.

Many Scots who had settled the Ulster Plantations in the seventeenth century later made the longer Atlantic crossing as Ulster-Scots. More than any other ethnic group, the Ulster-Scots accounted for the expansion of European settlement on the American frontier. Over 100,000 had settled in Pennsylvania by 1790: they then moved to the Carolinas and Georgia before heading west through the Cumberland Gap to Kentucky and Tennessee to become the classic backwoodsmen. Sometimes it is impossible to differentiate the place names with which they marked their exodus as being Scots or Ulster-Scots.

Trekking on

Melsetter, Zimbabwe, traces its rather tortuous roots to the first planned British immigration scheme in Cape Colony. The scheme was instigated by Captain Benjamin Moodie, 9th laird of Melsetter in Orkney, who brought out 200 Scottish artisans to settle the area in 1817.

Moodie may have taken the idea of an assisted passage scheme from Lieutenant-Colonel John Graham, who considered the best way to protect British interests against local tribes was to settle the eastern boundary of Cape Colony, which had been taken from the Dutch in 1806. Born in Fintry in Stirlingshire, he set up a military outpost at Grahamstown, which is now home to Rhodes University. While on home leave in 1813, Graham had taken soundings in the Highlands about interest in emigrating to Cape Colony.

Moodie pursued Graham's idea despite lack of encouragement from the British government. He recruited 200 candidates from more than 1,500 applicants, preferring young, single men of good character. He offered them apprenticeships either working on his own land or being hired out as labourers or craftsmen. Early in 1817 Moodie and his party sailed for the Cape via London on the *Brilliant*, the *Garland* and the *Clyde*. Sadly his experiment was short-lived. The promised financial support failed to materialise and the apprentices either failed to pay their debts or absconded for more profitable employment. In 1818 the family home in Orkney had to be sold.

Nonetheless Benjamin and his brother Donald thrived, Donald rising to become Colonial Secretary in Natal. Working for Cecil Rhodes' British South Africa Company in 1893, grandson Dunbar Moodie led a trek to open up Zimbabwe with the instruction to offer a farm to anyone in the Orange Free State prepared to trek east. Dunbar contacted his uncle, Thomas Moodie, a farmer in the State, who organised a party of 29 families, with 350 horses and cattle, to make the journey. Setting off in May 1892, they faced attacks by lions, a shortage of water, an outbreak of foot and mouth among the cattle, and desertion by many trekkers when they realised that they were not heading north to settled country around Salisbury. Only 21 people and seven wagons continued, having to dynamite their way through rock, hack through scrub, cross a mountain range, and endure malaria and horse sickness. Nine months later they reached green rolling hills where they settled, christening the area of Chipinga district Melsetter. Thomas Moodie did not live long to enjoy his new surroundings, dying less than a year later of black water fever.

William Ryrie faced the hazard of snakes rather than lions on his great trek across Australia. Born in 1805 in Caithness, he emigrated with his brothers around 1826, settling first in New South Wales. Then he and his family undertook a second immense journey, overlanding with four convict stockmen, 250 head of stock and some vine cuttings to plant Victoria's first vineyard on 43,000 acres bordered by the Yarra River. The name 'Yarra' is attributed to surveyor John Wedge, who, while on a reconnaissance expedition, asked local Aborigines what they called the cascading waters on the lower section of the river. They replied

'Yarro Yarro', meaning 'it flows'. Wedge misheard them and called it the Yarra.

Traders established themselves across the river at Yarra Flats to cater for settlers and gold prospectors who travelled the 'Yarra Track' to the Woods Point goldfields. After the arrival of the railway in 1888, the townspeople felt the need for a more desirable name and changed Yarra Flats to Yarra Glen.

Island hopping

Cape Breton Island, Nova Scotia, has a Gaelic name, Eilean Cheap Bhreatainn, and is often described as the Hebrides on the other side of the Atlantic. Benacadie, Boisdale, Ben Eoin, Sgurra Bhreac and Barra Glen are a few of the names that reflect the Scottish influence. Holiday homes now surround Loch Lomond Lake, recalling the ancestral lands of the MacAulays, who later moved to the Uists. In the late eighteenth century, it was the destination of more Hebridean Scots than any other part of the then British Empire.

Poet and seafarer Michael MacDonald was one of many Scots who moved from Prince Edward Island and Nova Scotia to Cape Breton Island, encouraging family and friends from home to join him in 1775 in the future Inverness County. The first emigrants were two MacNeil families from Barra, who came from Nova Scotia to prospect for land and settled in Iona. Enthused by a spirit of adventure, other families followed, settling on both sides of the Barra Strait, which connects the northern and southern basins of the Bras d'Or Lake in the centre of the island. People from South Uist began to arrive around 1793, some as over-spill from the increasingly settled Prince Edward Island. From 1820, the clearances in South Uist provided added impetus to emigration. As the original settlements became overcrowded, the younger generations moved again, some to the coal mines around Sydney and Glace Bay, but others to the fishing villages of the north. Under pressure from the failure of the kelp industry and lured by advertisements for fare-paying passengers to Nova Scotia, people from North Uist also made the journey. Most settled near their neighbours from home.

A very different type of immigrant arrived in the late nineteenth century, namely Lowland Scots attracted to work in Cape Breton's coal mines or as farmers. Finding conditions as tough as at home, many moved again to the cities, the mining areas of the western USA, the Canadian prairies or to the Antipodes. The descendants of the Cape Breton Scots are scattered throughout the globe. Those that stayed continue to celebrate their heritage in folk songs, storytelling and festivals on the island that describes itself as the 'Celtic Heart of North America'.

The same pattern of emigrating more than once also held true in the Antipodes. The area around Strathmore, Melbourne, was first settled in the 1830s, largely by emigrants sailing across the Bass Strait from Tasmania. One such settler was Thomas Napier from Montrose who settled initially in Hobart in 1832 as a builder before moving on to Melbourne five years later. He gradually acquired building plots, including 100 acres in the future community of Strathmore, where he built his own house, Rosebank. His son Theodore flew the flag for Scotland, having returned to the home country to train as a civil engineer. He regularly wore the kilt, and shoes with silver buckles, and carried a shepherd's crook. In 1891, he formed the Victorian Scottish Home Rule Association and each year raised the Saltire on his flag pole to mark the anniversary of the Battle of Bannockburn. He called his house Magdala in honour of the Abyssinian exploits in 1868 of his namesake, Sir Robert Napier. A benefactor to the district, he donated land for a public park, which was named in his honour.

By the 1930s, the area, known originally as North Essendon, was transforming itself from a farming community to suburbia. The construction of a second Presbyterian Church led the minister of both churches, John Sinclair, to suggest a name change to avoid confusion. He came up with Strathmore on two grounds – Strathmore was close to Thomas Napier's birthplace and it honoured Queen Elizabeth, as daughter of the Earl and Countess of Strathmore. People liked the name and it was adopted in 1933. Rejected names included Hendon, a combination of the name of the local Councillor William Henshall and the original Essendon.

Settling the borders

Emigration to Canada only really took off after the American Revolution, when Loyalists who had settled in America but fought with the British during the revolution moved across the border. The authorities offered land grants to former soldiers, many of whom were of Highland origin. By 1815, there were 15,000 Scots in Canada, many of whom were Gaelic speakers.

The history of St Andrews, New Brunswick, starts in 1783 when the group who became known as the Penobscot Loyalists from all over New England dismantled their houses and inns, piled them onto schooners or towed them behind their vessels, and sailed for St Andrews. The name St Andrews predated the arrival of the group. According to tradition, a French missionary had landed there on St Andrews Day, erected a cross, celebrated mass and named the location St André; by 1770, it had been anglicised to St Andrew's Point. The group of Loyalists had initially settled further down the coast until it became clear that the St Croix River rather than the Penobscot River was to define the international boundary between the USA and Canada. They then moved to St Andrews, a stone's throw over the border from Maine.

Their leader was Robert Pagan, the son of a Glasgow sugar refiner. His father set him up around 1768 in the expanding timber and shipbuilding trade of Falmouth, Massachusetts, with the aim of ultimately gaining a foothold in the lucrative West Indies trade. The Pagans were an entrepreneurial family. Robert's elder brother, William, was already apprenticed in the West Indies, while John was active in promoting Scottish immigration to Boston and Philadelphia. The youngest Pagan brother, Thomas, joined Robert in 1775 just before Falmouth was attacked by the rebel Americans. Suspected of Loyalist sympathies, the family fled to the West Indies.

On learning that a haven for Loyalists was to be established at the end of the war, three of the Pagan brothers returned first to the mouth of the Penobscot and then to St Andrews at the mouth of the St Croix. For a trading family, the situation was ideal, with its commercial links to Nova Scotia and the potential to develop the West Indies trade. Robert prospered, especially after his discovery that the local black birch was an effective and enduring wood for shipbuilding. He was so successful that for a time it looked as if St Andrews would surpass St John as New Brunswick's chief port. By the time of his death in 1820, he was one of the 12 wealthiest men in the province. In the late nineteenth century, St Andrews gained a new name – St Andrews-by-the-Sea – having been discovered as a seaside resort by wealthy individuals on both sides of the border.

At the other end of the USA, Eucheeanna was the first Scottish settlement in Florida. It was established by a group of Scots who had emigrated to North Carolina around 1810 but who decided a decade later to make a fresh start in Florida, which was in the throes of becoming US territory. Tipped off by Spanish merchants that the Euchee Valley would be a good place to settle, their leader Neil McLendon, who had gone ahead to prospect, met Sam Story, the chief of the Indian Euchee tribe. On Story's recommendation McLendon established a settlement across Bruce Creek from the tribe's headquarters. Respecting the Native American name, he called his settlement Eucheanna: it soon acquired a school, court house, jail, Masonic and Odd Fellows halls, general stores, a saw mill and a grain mill. Although the Scots and the Euchee Indians became friends, other white settlers in the area treated the Native Americans badly and in 1832 Story made a long trip to the Everglades to look for a new homeland. Shortly after he returned, exhausted and ill, he died. His Scottish friends buried him and erected a simple marker of heart pine – 'Sam Story, chief of the Euchees'.

Opening up the prairies

In the mid-nineteenth century, the opening up of the prairies of Western Ontario offered opportunities both for new emigrants and for those on the move from eastern Canada. The settlement of Bruce County, Western Ontario, around 1850 followed the typical pattern of surveying the land, dividing it into plots, building roads and attracting purchasers or tenants. Development along the roads was encouraged by the offer of free land provided the applicant was male, over 18 and a subject of Queen Victoria. Once they had cleared 12 of the 50 acres, settlers were entitled to buy the adjacent 50 acres at a nominal price. The first settlers and their oxen had to be tough to cope in the wilderness, where wolves, bears and lynx still roamed and marshes were crossed on 'corduroy roads' made of logs thrown over the swampy ground.

Bruce County took its name from James Bruce, 8th Earl of Elgin, who became Governor General of Canada in 1847. The first settlers named the townships after places associated with their roots or with their governor. All parts of Scotland were represented – Kincardine, Greenock, Arran, Kinloss, Elderslie, Carrick, Culross, Tobermory, Paisley, Solway, Lochalsh, Elgin, Dunkeld, Dunblane, Eskdale, Skipness, Bervie and Aberdour. One tiny settlement was even named Porridgeville because it had a grain mill.

Many of these settlements have since vanished from the map, having either been abandoned or subsumed into larger townships. Others, including Arran, Elderslie, Paisley and Kincardine, remain thriving communities today.

Some Ontario farmers then moved on to Michigan, as new opportunities arose. Alexander McLachlin established the first post office in Argyle, Michigan, in 1876, bringing with him the McLean and McIntyre families, while Kinross was named by Canadian farmers who had moved to Michigan.

West by road and rail

Improved communications played a vital role in opening up new territory, especially in Canada, where the authorities were keen to populate their empty lands – in part to create a stronger buffer against being taken over by the neighbouring USA. A typical story is that of the future town of Renfrew, Ontario. The first settlers along the Bonnechere River from the 1820s were farmers or timber workers. When the post office opened in 1848, they named their community Renfrewville, possibly after the ancestral homelands of the royal Stewarts. By 1854, the settlement boasted a blacksmith, a tannery, a shoemaker, a brewery, a doctor's office and a sawmill. In that year, the Opeongo Road, a colonisation initiative by the government to open up areas to settlement and timber production, arrived and a railway followed in 1872. Improved communication links resulted in a dramatic rise in immigration. To reflect this change, the village of Renfrewville became the town of Renfrew. Today, it is the regional centre for Ontario's largest county.

As emigrants flooded to the west of Canada, their first reminder of home was often the stopping point where they disembarked from the Canadian Pacific Railway (CPR). The CPR was empowered with naming the hamlets that sprang up at its sidings. Scotsman James Ross was in charge of the project and he tended to favour Scottish names. Strathmore, Alberta, was one such halt. It also turned out to be a record breaker when the construction squad laid a mile of track in an hour on 29 July 1883. Ross may have called the halt Strathmore after one of the CPR's backers, Claude Bowes-Lyon, Earl of Strathmore. His granddaughter passed through Strathmore in 1939 as the wife of King George VI.

Strathmore is known as 'the town that moved' because in 1905 it was decided to relocate it four miles north, thanks to the development of an irrigation system. Intensive advertising, both by the government and the CPR, had resulted in settlers from both the USA and 'the old country' pouring west.

The CPR sited its world-famous demonstration farm at Strathmore. It was designed to act as both a model and an instruction tool for settlers, many of whom had never farmed before. The farm grew vegetables and flowers for CPR dining cars and hotels, and experimented with growing exotic plants 'to make the area seem like a Shangri-La to the immigrants'. The last rail of the siding was only removed in 1981.

Over the years, the CPR's network spread its tentacles over the land. After surveying the area in 1912, it decided to build a line in the rural corner of south-west Saskatchewan, along the Frenchman River. By then a few homesteaders had put down roots as wheat growers. A CPR official named the settlement Ravenscrag after the Italianate mansion built in Montreal in 1863 by Sir Hugh Allan, the Saltcoats-born son of the founder of the Allan shipping line that carried many Scottish emigrants to Canada. The CPR had purchased the Allan Line in 1917. The hamlet, in turn, gave its name to a local geological feature, the Ravenscrag Formation, part of the Western Canadian Sedimentary Basin. The community struggled to survive the Depression and a major fire in 1954. The last grain elevator was demolished in the 1980s and fewer than 20 people now live in Ravenscrag, all but one belonging to the same family.

The CPR received vast areas of land under its railway construction contract: these were to be settled and sold for revenue. Once its rail network was complete, the CPR started to promote Western Canada as the 'Wondrous West'. Working with Father Andrew MacDonell, it organised immigrants into groups, providing them with a free passage and basic provisions, and lending them funds to purchase land. The Clandonald Colony in Alberta was a typical settlement of immigrant families brought over from the Hebrides in 1926.

Railway companies in general were faced with the challenge of naming their stations, from remote halts to railroad towns. While some like the CPR took this task seriously, others left it rather more to chance. The naming of Glasgow, Montana, began with a spin of the globe. Its original name was simply Siding 45, the 45th siding west of Minot, North Dakota, on the Great Northern Railway's Hi-Line. Starting in Montana in 1887 and averaging 5 to 8 miles of track-laying a day, the railroad reached the Pacific six years later. The story goes that, with hundreds of stations to name, the railway officials resorted to spinning a globe and pointing with a finger: Glasgow was one such random choice. The railroad brought thousands of ranchers and farmers into Montana and transported out the crops they grew. A new influx of people arrived from the late 1950s to the huge Glasgow Air Force Base, which at its peak employed 16,000 personnel.

Perth, North Dakota, was founded in 1897 as a prairie town by R. J. Laird at the time of the building of the Great Northern Railroad. It was named Perth by a Scots member of the railroad crew. It was lucky for Aberdeen, South Dakota, that the man in charge, Charles Prior, knew its name. As superintendent of the Minneapolis office of the proposed Chicago Milwaukee and St Paul Railroad, his job was to plot the route and identify places for new towns along the line. He chose the names after places or people he knew. He selected Aberdeen as a town site in 1881, naming it after his boss, Alexander Mitchell, who was born in Aberdeen, Scotland. On 6 July, the first Milwaukee Railroad train steamed into town. With three railroads crossing at Aberdeen, the development proved popular with land speculators, businessmen, fortune seekers and adventurers. Aberdeen expanded rapidly to become the third-largest city in South Dakota.

SIC TRANSIT GLORIA MUNDI

Especially in North America, people tended to keep on the move as economic circumstances changed and new opportunities arose. Today, the only sign that a thriving community once existed is a scattering of ruined buildings, rusting railroad tracks or a roadside plaque recording the former community's history. Maps are marked simply with the name of the place and 'abandoned settlement' or 'ghost town'.

Two of Canada's three Dunblanes are categorised as ghost towns.

Dunblane, Bruce County, Ontario, was settled in the early 1850s. The heart of a farming community, it soon boasted a post office, an inn, a store, a church, a sawmill, a blacksmith, a weaver and a veterinarian – and eventually a school. The village spelled its name both as Dumblane and Dunblane. The closure of the mill, and then the school, was the death knell of the village, although the unused church still survives as a designated historic structure.

The first known rancher in the area around Dunblane, Saskatchewan, was one Robert Cruickshank and other Scots settlers followed, giving rise to more home country names such as Birsay and Glenside. While watching the settlers struggle to plough the infertile land, one local cowboy is reported to have commented: 'By Gawd, boy, why don't you buy a cow and watch her grow!'

By the time the Canadian National Railway came to Dunblane in 1914, the town had acquired its name. In 1920, it boasted a hotel with two VIP suites for travelling salesmen, several stores, a café, a poolroom, a telephone exchange and a Ford car dealership. Three trainloads of crude oil rumbled through Dunblane daily until the trans-Canadian pipeline was built, reducing train services to one a week. The influx of workers building the Gardiner Dam from 1959 provided a brief lifeline to the village. Houses were then moved to new locations and commercial buildings were demolished for their materials. By 1980 little remained but a station name sign with the legend 'Dunblane'.

Other examples include:

Cameron Falls, Ontario – a hydroelectric town near Cameron Lake, named after early settler Duncan Cameron. When the plant was automated in the 1960s, employees could purchase their homes if they moved them.

Lochalsh, Ontario – a CPR railway station that expanded into a bustling town when gold was discovered in the 1920s. Lochalsh once boasted two hotels and a Chinese restaurant: with the closure of the mines, the population moved away.

St Boswells, Saskatchewan – called after the Scottish home of the settlement's first postmaster, Alex Gray. With its grain elevators typical of the prairie landscape, the railway town flourished until the stock market crash and the 1930s Depression hit hard. Now a grassy track is the only reminder of busy Main Street.

Lochiel, Arizona – named in 1884 by the cattle baron Colin Cameron after his clan homeland, the town grew up to serve the neighbouring ranches and mines, and as a border crossing with Mexico. The settlement was abandoned in the 1980s.

Carnegie, California – a brick-making factory and town, named by the owner in 1902 after his entrepreneurial hero. Less than two decades later, the plant was abandoned after a bank failure and floods. Two of California's Carnegie libraries are built of Carnegie bricks. Today, the site is a state vehicle recreation park.

Scotia, Pennsylvania – named by Andrew Carnegie in 1881 after his first large-scale iron-ore operation. Carnegie himself was a regular visitor to the village of around 250 families, where he enjoyed watching baseball games. The factory closed under a later owner and the village was abandoned by the 1920s.

Argyle, Utah – named by its Scots-American residents in 1885, the village declined after improved transport meant that ranchers no longer needed to live close to their fields. Today, all that remains is a boarded-up cabin.

Mossgiel, New South Wales – named by an early Burns enthusiast after the poet's Ayrshire farm. All that remains of this farming township is the former schoolhouse and a community centre.

Kelso, New Zealand – named after his home town by an early settler, Kelso was planned as the main township of West Otago. Despite being prone to floods, Kelso had a population of 300 in the 1960s; however, more inundations in the late 1970s convinced the authorities that the settlement was no longer viable. Today, all that remains is a plaque recording its history.

5

'Stopping here on their way to heaven'

This is how the American writer Mark Twain summed up his visit to Dunedin in New Zealand in the mid-1890s: 'The people here are Scots. They stopped here on their way to heaven, thinking they had arrived.' His comment could apply to several communities throughout the world. Wherever they settled, emigrants took the 'good book' with them. Religion drove some Scots to do more than find solace in the Bible and the family tree inscribed on its flyleaf. Whether as a result of persecution at home, the zeal to convert others or the desire to create a new Zion, Scots left their mark in the names they chose for their new communities.

The earliest examples of Scots taking their religion overseas arose not from the desire to convert others but from the need to escape persecution. For Covenanters and Roman Catholics alike, emigration offered the opportunity to practise their chosen faith freely. Opening up areas to trade and the resulting contact with native people brought pressure to establish missions. In the nineteenth century, having a foreign mission branch was almost a status symbol for the growing number of Scottish church denominations. The earliest missionary societies in Scotland were founded in 1796, namely the Scottish Society and the Glasgow Society for Foreign Missions. Representing Church of Scotland and Secession Church interests, their early evangelical activity embraced West Africa, the Caribbean, the Caucasus and India.

Gradually, mainstream church organisations took over these early missions. After pressure mounted for a missionary society run directly by the Church of Scotland, in 1829 the General Assembly dispatched Alexander Duff, its first overseas missionary, to Calcutta. He set up the General Assembly's Institution and, following his transfer of allegiance, the Free Church Institution. The two institutions were the progenitors of the Scottish Church College, whose students and alumni still call themselves Caledonians. In 1845, the Free Church of Scotland formed its own Foreign Missions Board, which assumed responsibility for the South African stations of the Glasgow Missionary Society. Similarly, in 1847 the new United Presbyterian Church took over the Scottish Missionary Society's Jamaica and Calabar (Nigerian) missions. Activity gathered pace from the 1850s, in the Punjab, Poona, the Eastern Himalayas, Blantyre in Malawi, Yichang in China, Kikuyu in Kenya and Iringa in Tanzania.

The type of missionary work undertaken varied. While the work pioneered in India by Alexander Duff was firmly rooted in education, many African missions placed more emphasis on treating and eradicating disease. Missionaries were among the first Europeans to open up the interior of regions such as Southern Africa. Their motives were genuine and high-minded. They introduced education, healthcare and improved farming techniques as well as religion to local populations. Arguably these practical improvements had more influence on the spiritual as well as physical well-being of local people than sermons from the pulpit and attempts to impose moral standards alien to native culture and traditions. While many missions came and went without trace, some adopting local names or now surviving only as churches or schools, some missionaries left a more permanent mark.

Individuals also set up their own Zions, founding communities according to their own beliefs and running them according to their own moral code. Although many of these settlements were short-lived, depending on the charisma or autocratic power of their leader to hold the faithful together, a few left a more permanent legacy in their place name.

Seeking freedom to practise their faith

Stuart's Town, South Carolina, owes its origin to the coming together in the 1660s of a young colony seeking settlers and a group of Scottish Covenanters escaping oppression. The Carolina Proprietors wanted to establish a second settlement south of Charleston to act as a buffer against hostile Native Americans and Spaniards. After defeat at the Battle of Bothwell Bridge, a group of influential Scottish lairds led by Sir John Cochran of Ochiltree and Sir George Campbell negotiated the purchase of two counties to be settled by Scottish Covenanters in 1682. The findings of an exploratory expedition promoted the new counties in *A New and Most Exact Account of the Fertiles and Famous Colony of Carolina.*

The *Carolina Merchant* sailed from Greenock in 1684 with 149 passengers, including 35 convicts on board; a second ship, the *Malloch*, carrying 150 Scottish prisoners from Belfast, foundered. Fever reduced the number of colonists who set off down the coast from Charleston to 51. They named their chosen site Stuart's Town in honour of Catherine Stuart Erskine, the wife of one of the leaders. The colony was short-lived. The Spanish set fire to the town in 1686, by which time the number of Scots fit to fight had been reduced to 25. Some returned to Scotland and others settled elsewhere in South Carolina. Few traces of Stuart's Town remain, other than the town seal, now a prized possession of the Carolina Library Society, and Stuart's Town Road in the city of Beaufort.

Scottish Quakers had more luck in establishing Perth Amboy and other settlements in New Jersey. A charter of 1683 granted the colony of New Jersey, divided into East and West, to 24 proprietors, 12 of whom were Scots and most of whom were Quakers. There were six Scottish Quakers among the East Jersey proprietors, including George Scott of Pitlochie, Robert Gordon of Gordonstoun and Robert Barclay of Urie. The group elected Barclay first governor of New Jersey, although he never set foot in America.

Although not personally persecuted, Barclay was aware of hostility towards Quakers in the north-east of Scotland and saw a colony as a refuge but not an exclusive Quaker enclave. He encouraged his relatives and fellow countrymen to emigrate to enjoy religious freedom. In 1685 Scott was permitted to emigrate provided he took with him more than a hundred Covenanters – at the time imprisoned in Leith Tolbooth – as bonded labour. The party set sail from Leith in the *Francis* and the *Henry*. During a 15-week crossing, Scott, his wife and over half the passengers, many of whom had been weakened by imprisonment in Dunnottar Castle, died of fever. Of the survivors, some purchased land on the banks of Matawan Creek, calling the settlement New Aberdeen.

The community had to wait three centuries before the name Aberdeen was officially adopted. In the eighteenth century, as the settlement expanded along the creek, local traders opted to call it Middletown Point. Then to avoid confusion with nearby Middletown, Middletown Point changed its name to Matawan in 1865. To re-establish its local identity and put it at the head of the New Jersey alphabet, the original Aberdeen declared its 'independence' from Matawan in 1977 and became Aberdeen again.

The 700 Scots, mostly from the north-east, who emigrated to East Jersey in the 1680s found the land fertile, the climate kind and West Jersey to be a harmonious neighbour. Until 1697 every governor of East Jersey was Scottish, and Scots proved influential in politics and business even after East and West Jersey merged to become a Royal Colony in 1702, with Perth Amboy as one of the two capitals.

Linguistically 'Amboy' had travelled far from the original Native American name, Ompoge, meaning 'level ground' to Emboyle, Amboyle, Ambo and finally Amboy, the name that it was known by at the time of its incorporation in 1718. Perth was not the home town of one of the settlers but was called after the Earl of Perth, one of the original New Jersey Proprietors and Lord High Chancellor under King James II. A century and a half later, Perth Amboy was a major industrial centre, attracting immigrants from all over Europe who christened their new neighbourhoods, such as Dublin and Budapest.

The name of the city of McKeesport, Pennsylvania, comes from David McKee, born in Scotland in 1710. His parents were strict Presbyterians, serious-minded and deeply religious. They escaped first to Northern Ireland and then America in search of a 'church without a bishop and a state without a king'. In 1769, McKee and two of his sons applied to purchase land to farm near Pittsburgh. Despite their religious scruples, they made whiskey on the side. The McKees also operated the first ferryboats across the Monongahela and Youghiogheny rivers. In 1781, David transferred his land to his son John, the founder of the future city. John cleared the land and sold it in parcels, donating four lots for a school and a church. In 1795 the *Pittsburgh Gazette* carried the announcement: 'A NEW TOWN is laid out by the subscriber on a spot known for many years past by the name of McKee's Ferry.'

The next year the new name McKees Port was adopted to avoid confusion with two other settlements also calling themselves McKee's Ferry.

Although the McKee fortune dwindled, the discovery of natural gas, the establishment of coal mines, and the founding of iron and steel industries resulted in the rapid growth of the community in the late nineteenth century.

More than half a century after the foundation of McKeesport, the Black family briefly settled there. William Black from the Glasgow area and his Islay-born wife Isabella Neilson had boarded the *Affghan* for Boston in 1847, travelling with six children whose ages ranged from 19 to a ten-month-old granddaughter. A year later the Blacks moved six miles upriver, where a village soon grew up around their farm. Homesick William had named the farm Greenock, reminding him of his last sight of Scotland.

Glengarry County, Ontario, was the result of a different faith seeking to practise its beliefs unimpeded by the authorities. Although the celebration of mass had been banned since the Reformation, pockets of Roman Catholicism remained, especially in the remoter parts of the Highlands. After the defeat of the Jacobites at Culloden in 1746, emigration was increasingly the only option and it is estimated that a quarter of Roman Catholics in the Highlands had emigrated by 1790. Between 1773 and 1853 nearly 3,500 people from Lochiel, Glengarry, Knoydart and Glenelg settled in Glengarry County.

Led by three MacDonnel brothers who were originally tacksmen on the Glengarry Estate, the first settlers were soldiers who had fought for the British in the American Revolutionary Wars. From 1784, they were joined by friends and relatives who organised five sailings from Scotland. During the brief peace of 1802, during the Napoleonic Wars, close to a thousand clansmen emigrated to Glengarry. They included Father Alexander MacDonnell and his 500-strong flock, many of whom had been evicted from Glengarry in one of the early Clearances: he applied to the British government for a large land grant in what became

Glengarry County. In 1815, the last large group of emigrants left western Inverness-shire for a new life in the region. The area round Williamstown was popular with fur-trade veterans of the North West Company.

The settlers built rough log shanties, began clearing the land of oaks and elms, and survived the winter cold and the summer insects. Father Alexander MacDonnel actively promoted education and Catholicism in his adopted land, founding the College of Iona at St Raphael's to train men for the priesthood. He ended his career in 1826 as the first Bishop of Upper Canada, with his see at Kingston. Glengarry County is proud of its Scottish roots, the annual Glengarry Highland Games claiming to be the largest outside Scotland. Canada's first Clan MacLeod Society was founded there in 1936.

Practising what they preached

A group of Scots chose Dunedin, Otago, New Zealand, on the other side of the world in which to found their New Edinburgh Settlement run according to their own religious and moral beliefs. The secular leader of the expedition, which set out in 1847, was Captain William Cargill and its spiritual leader was the Reverend Thomas Burns, a nephew of the poet.

William Cargill was only 15 when his father, an Edinburgh lawyer, died of alcoholism, leaving the family in straitened circumstances. Like his strong-minded mother, William was influenced by the preacher Thomas Chalmers, who shaped much of his thinking about society. He found employment in the army, as a wine merchant and in banking, as well as starting a family of 17 children. By the early 1840s, he had become interested in emigration. He approached George Rennie, the Scottish politician, sculptor and dreamer, who promised him a leading role in any Scots settlement in New Zealand. The Disruption of 1843 helped to identify a body of prospective colonists, and Rennie and Cargill approached the leaders of the new Free Church of Scotland, who backed their proposals.

Born near Mauchline, Ayrshire, in 1796, Thomas Burns and his deeply pious farming family moved to East Lothian. After studying theology at Edinburgh University, Burns enjoyed two comfortable livings in Ayrshire before 'coming out' in 1843 and accepting a greatly reduced standard of living as a minister of the Free Church of Scotland. He was appointed minister to the proposed settlement. Four long years of negotiation passed before the emigrants were ready to sail. Burns, who was forced to take up a new ministry in Portobello to make ends meet, persuaded Cargill to drop Rennie, establish an exclusively Free Church settlement and to change the name of the colony from New Edinburgh to Otago. He travelled the length and breadth of Scotland promoting the scheme and recruiting emigrants with limited success. A land agent selected the site of the future Dunedin and Port Chalmers in Otago Harbour, an area rarely visited by Europeans except for occasional whalers and sealers.

Burns, his family and 239 emigrants set sail on the *Philip Laing* from Greenock on 27 November 1847. Cargill had already left from Gravesend three days earlier with 96 emigrants on board the *John Wickliffe*. The voyage revealed Burns' true colours. He held daily services, rising to three on Sundays, and policed the morals of younger emigrants who viewed him at best as an Old Testament patriarch. They landed at the future Port Chalmers, which they named after the theologian who had so influenced Cargill, who gave a rousing speech, comparing his shipload to the Pilgrim Fathers.

The first year was not easy. A harsh winter hampered laying down essentials such as roads and much of the land proved unsuitable for arable farming. Grain from Burns' farm helped the settlers to survive. There was constant bickering between the Scots and English, not helped by Cargill's own intransigent views on the Anglican religion. By the end of 1848, however, the *Otago News* was able to report:

> On every side a wilderness of wood, flax and fern met the eye . . . now instead of seeing one or two solitary houses, with a narrow swampy footpath, the eye is gladdened with a goodly sprinkling of houses, some of wood, others of mud and grass; whilst numerous gardens, well fenced and cleared, and one street, at least showing a broad track from end to end of the future town, gives evidence of the progress we have made.

By then Otago had two hotels, a church, a school, a wharf, a butcher's, a baker's and general stores.

Cargill was elected superintendent of the province in 1853. His personal style, epitomised by his dress of a blue bonnet and tartan plaid, amused English observers, infuriated government officials and made the autocratic old soldier very popular among the Scots. Within Otago he ruled with an iron fist, promoting his relatives and dismissing the provincial council if it dared to criticise his policies. The Otago of the late 1850s, however, was a far cry from the ideals of its founders. It had attracted labourers rather than men of substance as settlers. Drunken and uncouth behaviour were widespread, although Cargill managed to hold the settlement together. His death in 1860 was timely: soon thousands of rough but democratically minded gold miners put paid to the last shreds of his dream of the Pilgrim Fathers. With the discovery of gold, Dunedin prospered, becoming New Zealand's largest city by 1900.

When the godless gold miners arrived, Thomas Burns was forced to take a more lenient line on religion on the grounds that any Christian faith was better than none. From the start, he had left the practical organisation of the new settlement to Cargill, busying himself by visiting each family on a regular basis to attend to their spiritual needs and by extending the work of the church to rural areas. Once he realised that many settlers were not Free Church members, he abandoned his ideal of creating a new Geneva and opposing the presence of other denominations – he had initially forced the Anglicans to worship in the gaol.

Before his death in 1871, Burns was proud to become the first Chancellor of the University of Otago, whose buildings were modelled on those of Glasgow University. Burns' farming background also led to the foundation of Mosgiel, now a suburb of Dunedin. He selected the land in 1849, naming it after his uncle Robert's farm in Ayrshire, which a few years later his son Arthur started to work.

Today, Dunedin – known as the 'Athens of the South' – shares many of the features of its Scottish sister, 'the Athens of the North'. The main thoroughfares are Princes Street and George Street; there is Heriot Row, Waverley Station and Murrayfield rugby stadium. The city draws much of its water from a reservoir fed by the Water of Leith. The first Burns Supper was held only five years after the Scottish settlers arrived and Dunedin also holds an annual Scottish week, which includes crowning the Queen o' the Heather, Kirkin' o' the Tartan, tossing the caber and consuming haggis patties. The city even has its own registered tartan, the Dunedin District of New Zealand.

Cargill separately earned a place in the atlas in the name Invercargill, the southernmost and westernmost city in New Zealand, and one of the most southerly settlements in the world. Once the Scots had settled the Otago region, in 1856 they petitioned the governor for a port at Bluff. The governor agreed and called the settlement north of the port Invercargill. Many of Invercargill's streets are named after Scottish rivers, including Dee, Esk, Don, Ness, Yarrow, Spey and Tay. Even today people in the area are said to have traces of Scottish speech, notably the rolling burr of the 'R'.

The mission to convert

The towns of Aberdeen, Alexandria, Fraserburg, McGregor, Murraysburg, Robertson and Sutherland all honour Scottish Calvinists who became Dutch Reformed Church ministers soon after South Africa's Cape region became a British possession in 1806. The Scots had already been active as explorers. The first person to map the area was Dutch-born Captain Robert Jacob Gordon, whose father had been in the Scots Brigade. He travelled with William Paterson, the Montrose-born botanist who from 1777 explored deep into the interior, thanks to the patronage of Lady Strathmore.

The missionaries were not long in arriving. Campbell, Northern Cape, was one of the earliest centres of Christianity north of the Orange River. Originally Grootfontein, or Knoffelvallei, the town was renamed to honour the Reverend John Campbell, traveller and missionary, who visited the Cape stations of the London Missionary Society in 1813. Orphaned at an early age, Campbell was brought up by his uncle, a pious Edinburgh elder. A contributor to *Tait's Edinburgh Magazine* wrote of him in 1840: 'His restless temperament and enterprising spirit were more inclined to action than study, and might have led him headlong into evil, had they not been kept in check by the wholesome restraints and religious education established in his uncle's household.' Apprenticed to a goldsmith, Campbell became a city missionary among 'the murky lanes and closes' and was active in setting up Sabbath schools and preaching stations throughout central Scotland.

It was an easy step for Campbell to become a missionary initially as the Edinburgh director of the London Missionary Society. Campbell persuaded it to send him on a tour of exploration through 'Caffraria' in 1812 to revive the society's Hottentot and Caffre missions. He covered over 3,000 miles in the next two years. He returned to the Cape from 1818, touring mission stations before resuming his ministerial duties at Kingsland Chapel in London.

By mid-century, parish ministers were taking the place of missionaries. Fraserburg, Northern Cape, is a hybrid of the names of the Scottish cleric the Reverend Colin Fraser and church elder G. J. Meyburg. In 1851, Fraser helped set up the new Dutch Reformed Church parish to serve the growing number of farmers. He went on to establish the first church in the Orange Free State at Philippolis in 1863.

Aberdeen was founded in 1855 when the Dutch Reformed Church of Graaff-Reinet gave permission for the establishment of a new congregation. The farm Brakfontein was bought for the purpose in 1860. In the same year the name of the settlement around Brakfontein was changed to Aberdeen, the birthplace of the minister Dr Andrew Murray. The church was not completed until 1907 by which time the town had grown wealthy on the ostrich feather trade. The spire is nicknamed 'the leaning tower of Aberdeen': as well as being the tallest in South Africa, it is 18 inches off centre. Nestling in the Western Cape's 'valley of wine and roses', Robertson is named after a Scottish Dutch Reformed Church Minister, Dr William Robertson. Among his parish ports of call was the home of farmer Johannes W. van Zijl, where he held a service every three months. When it was decided in 1852 to found a new town, van Zijl's land was purchased and Robertson honoured.

Born on his father's farm near Inverurie, Aberdeenshire, in 1805, Robertson had to abandon his studies when he contracted TB. About the same time the governor of the Cape Colony was seeking to improve education and address the shortage of qualified ministers in the Dutch Reformed Church. He looked to Scotland for assistance. Aged only 17, Robertson set sail on the four-month journey to South Africa in 1822. His first posting was to Graaff-Reinet, where he opened the Free English School. His health much improved, he travelled back to Aberdeen to complete his training as a minister. Returning to South Africa in 1831, he served as a minister at Clanwilliam and Swellendam in between visits to Scotland on recruitment drives. He also found time to father ten children.

One of Robertson's recruits in 1860 was Andrew McGregor, whose father ran a shop called the Emporium in Golspie, Sutherland. At the time McGregor was minister of the Free Tolbooth Church in Edinburgh. He spent the rest of his career administering to the souls of Robertson Parish, following his mentor's example in fathering ten children. On his retirement in 1902 he moved to a house in Cape Town, which he named Rob Roy Villa. McGregor had also been very active in a neighbouring parish in the farming town of Lady Grey, originally named after the wife of a Cape governor. As a result of his work, this parish became a separate congregation in its own right and the village was renamed McGregor in his honour in 1906.

Sutherland, Northern Cape, took its name from Reverend Henry Sutherland, a Dutch Reformed Church minister born in Paisley. The town was laid out in 50 plots around 1857, receiving an annual pastoral visit from its namesake. Today, Sutherland is famous as being the coldest place in South Africa and for housing the Southern African Large Telescope (SALT), the largest single optical telescope in the southern hemisphere.

Lovedale was the original name of the town of Alice in South Africa's Eastern Cape until renamed in honour of Queen Victoria's second daughter, Princess Alice of Hesse. The name Lovedale was chosen not because it was a 'happy valley' but to honour John Love, the secretary of the Glasgow Missionary Society, which founded the station in 1824. Established in 1841, the Lovedale Mission Institute flourished under its second headmaster, James Stewart. He was a firm believer in practical training, teaching students how to build roads, dams and irrigation systems. He made no distinction regarding the sex or colour of students. The institute flourished, embracing the spectrum of education from primary, secondary and technical schools to teacher training and theological colleges. From 1916, Lovedale formed the basis of the University of Fort Hare – the first in Africa open to non-white students – which counts former presidents of South Africa Nelson Mandela and Thabo Mbeki among its alumni.

James Stewart did not confine his activities to the Eastern Cape. In 1870, he established the Gordon Memorial Mission at Umsinga in Natal. This meant riding a thousand miles over very rough country, sleeping anywhere he could persuade people to put him up for the night. He named the mission after the Honorable James Gordon, brother of the Earl of Aberdeen, whose untimely death in 1868 ruled out his ambition of working as a missionary in South Africa. The earl's family resolved to found a mission among the Zulus in his memory, entrusting it to the Free Church of Scotland. The names of Stewart's other mission stations also reflect their Scottish roots – Burnshill, Blythswood and Macfarlane.

The inspiration behind Stewart's decision to take up mission work was reading David Livingstone's *Missionary Travels and Researches in*

South Africa. While raising funds among evangelical businessmen to form the New Central African Mission Committee, Stewart met Mary Livingstone. She persuaded him to accompany her on the long journey to be reunited with her husband on the Zambezi. The nature of their relationship has been the subject of speculation ever since. Although Mary died two months after their arrival, Stewart stayed with the Livingstone expedition for 15 months. In 1874, while attending David Livingstone's funeral, Stewart started to fund-raise for the Livingstonia Mission to Nyasaland. Livingstonia is one of two settlements whose names reflect David Livingstone's historic visit to the future Malawi in 1859. Unlike many missionaries, he recognised that 'sending the Gospel to the heathen' meant much more than 'a man going about with a Bible under his arm'. His solution to eradicating the slave trade was to introduce the three Cs: Christianity, Commerce and Civilisation. Stewart took up the challenge of delivering Livingstone's vision of 'a colony of good Christian Scotch families'.

Now Malawi's second-largest city, Blantyre was named after Livingstone's humble birthplace on the outskirts of Glasgow. The settlement grew out of the Church of Scotland's Blantyre Mission, founded in 1876. St Michael and All Angels, the first permanent Christian church between the Zambezi and the Nile, was built by the Edinburgh-born head of the mission, the Reverend David Scott, and a local labour force. Without architectural or construction expertise, Scott built a brick edifice with domes, a tower and flying buttresses that still graces the city. It is a tribute to Livingstone's humanity and his efforts to abolish the slave trade in East Africa that in the post-colonial era place names honouring him in Malawi – as well as Livingstone in Zambia – have not been changed.

Scots missionaries were willing to take the Bible into the wildest outposts. Although its modern name is Inozemtsevo, older maps still feature the name Shotlandskaya Koloniya, 'the Scottish colony', in the Northern Caucasus. In 1802, Tsar Alexander I gave permission to Scottish missionaries 'to propagate Christianity to the tribes' in the hope of converting them from Islam. Among the missionaries were men with remarkable skills. Scholar and linguist the Reverend Henry Brunton translated the 'Tartar-Turkish' New Testament, operated a printing press, and was planning to develop a new alphabet and grammar for the Kabardian language when he died in 1813. James Galloway was a weaver as well as a missionary. He married a local woman and was allowed to remain when in 1835 Tsar Nicholas I suppressed the activities of the mission station. As a whole the venture was not a success. The group, which never exceeded 30 settlers, survived by farming and by buying and rearing enslaved children. They were regularly attacked by the tribes they had come to convert.

The story has a remarkable afterword. During his sojourn in Russia in the 1870s, Scots-born traveller and journalist Sir Donald Mackenzie Wallace sought out the site of the Scottish colony. There he met a 'Scotch Circassian' who informed him that his name was John Abercrombie and that among the many dialects he spoke was Lowland Scots. John was one of the local children adopted by the missionaries. They may have made few converts, but they left the mark of Scottish identity.

Support from a distance

A village in Rwanda has been renamed Dumbarton in honour of the parishioners of Dumbarton's Rock Community Church who raised about £30,000 for a variety of projects in the village previously known as Jari. The project was in response to the 1994 Rwandan genocide, which left 800,000 people dead.

Since 2008 church members have been engaged in helping the 150-strong Jari population. They have supplied agricultural products and sewing machines to provide work, and have bought land to build homes for widows and genocide survivors. Similar relationships have been built up by other Scottish and African congregations. The settlement of Pirie in South Africa's Eastern Cape is based around the Pirie Mission, which is now partnered with St Columba's Parish Church, Blackhall, in Edinburgh. The Reverend John Ross of the Glasgow Missionary Society founded Pirie in 1830, naming it after the society's first chairman, the Reverend Alexander Pirie. By mid-century, Pirie had a population of 5,700 housed in 165 homesteads called *kraals*.

Edina, Liberia, bears witness to the fact that congregations did not need to leave their pews but simply put money in the collection box in order to earn their place on the map. From 1820, several colonisation societies sent shiploads of freed slaves to the West African coast. Under the auspices of the American Colonization Society, one group from South Carolina established a farming settlement at the mouth of the St John's River in 1832. They called it Edina in thanks for the generosity of the people of Edinburgh in contributing money to the society. The community thrived, and soon acquired a school, two churches and a mission station. Today, it is the country's oldest city.

Travelling in the name of the Lord

Xenia, Ohio, was founded in 1803, the year that the state was admitted into the Union. The following year landowner Joseph Vance called a town meeting to choose a name for the new village in typically democratic fashion. Several options were bounced around without a conclusion emerging. The Reverend Robert Armstrong – described as a 'traveller' – then proposed

Xenia, from the classical Greek word for 'hospitality', because of the welcome extended to him in this friendly community. When the vote resulted in a tie, Laticia Davis, wife of the host of the meeting, leading townsman Owen Davis, was invited to cast the deciding ballot. She opted for Xenia.

The obliging 'traveller', the Reverend Robert Armstrong, left Scotland in 1792 with William Fulton as a Secession Church missionary. Armstrong described his travels in a letter home:

> I first provided myself with a large wallet, one end contains food for myself, the other end contains food for my horse, and my Indian blanket and my saddle bags, these are all fixed on the horse with the saddle. Some of your proud Scotch ministers will exclaim, 'travel in this mean style!' But this is the way all classes of men travel in this country.

James Galloway, one of the first settlers of Greene County, Ohio, had heard Armstrong preach while on surveying business in Kentucky. He persuaded Armstrong and his Kentucky congregations, who were opposed to slavery, to relocate to the fertile region around the future Xenia in 1804. Armstrong built himself a cabin and farm, and helped to erect a church at Massie's Creek, now part of Xenia. People walked up to 12 miles, even in winter, to hear his two Sunday sermons. A Seceder congregation was organised in Xenia itself in 1814. One wonders what Armstrong would have thought of the present-day pronunciation – Xeen-yuh – by the city's 24,000 residents.

The name Afton travelled from Ayrshire to Wyoming by a circuitous route. From the early 1840s, more than 300,000 emigrants headed west through the state on the Oregon Trail. Increased traffic led to the creation of the first federally funded road in the west – the Lander Cut-Off – built in 1858 and so-called because it reduced the journey for wagon trains by seven days. Many of the men recruited to build the road were Mormon emigrants from Salt Lake City, some of whom settled nearby using the pastures as summer grazing. In 1879, the area became Star Valley. The story goes that the Mormons originally christened it 'Starvation Valley' because of the long, harsh winters in the area, which is over 6,000 feet above sea level. Over time Starvation became shortened to Star. Others claim that it was known as the 'Star of All Valleys' because of its natural beauty.

It was decided to create a new settlement at the mouth of the Swift Creek Canyon. Born in Lanark and brought up in Glasgow, William Budge was a Mormon pioneer and friend of Brigham Young, a leader of the Mormon Church. He suggested that the new town be called Afton because the roaring, tumbling stream gushing through the canyon was the antithesis of the placid stream he remembered from the Burns' song 'Sweet Afton'. Incorporated in 1902, Afton grew quickly to have a population of over 2,000. Today, its claim to fame is that its Main Street is spanned by the world's largest elk horn arch, made of more than 3,000 antlers.

The deserts of Utah have attracted religious movements, the most famous of which is the Mormons. EskDale was the result of a splinter group, the House of Aaron, who established a community at EskDale on the border with Nevada in 1955. Maurice Glendenning, who saw visions and heard angelic voices as a child, founded the sect in 1942 after breaking away from the Mormon Church because of religious differences. He then followed the biblical injunction interpreted by one of his followers as 'to go into the land of the earth and build a place in an effort to live together'. Glendenning named the community EskDale because his ancestors hailed from Eskdale in Dumfriesshire.

Elgin, Illinois, was predestined to become Elgin, as was Dundee, New York State. They did not reflect the homeland roots of US pioneer James Gifford but the metrical psalm tunes that he carried in his head. He farmed in the area originally known as Harpending's Corners. When residents sought to change it to something more appealing in 1833, the suggestion of Plainville proved controversial and Gifford came up with the psalm tune 'Dundee'. By then, lured by tales of the fertile soils of Illinois, the deeply religious James and his younger brother, Hezekiah, were already planning to found a new settlement and give it the name Elgin. James wrote: 'I had been a great admirer of that tune from boyhood and the name Elgin had ever fallen upon my ear with musical effect.' After two months on the road, resting their wagon and horses on the Sabbath, the Giffords reached Elgin in 1835. James immediately returned east for his wife, children and relatives, the party floating down the Erie Canal to Buffalo, where they picked up a lake schooner. On arrival at Elgin, baby Sarah was lifted from the wagon and immediately plonked herself down on the floor: she was declared to be Elgin's first real settler. James's log cabin served as the church on the following Sunday. From such modest beginnings, Elgin grew to become Illinois' eighth-largest city.

Utopia

Perhaps the strangest example of Scots missionary zeal is Zion, Illinois. Evangelist John Alexander Dowie was a man with a very personal mission, which he realised by founding Zion in 1900. He claimed that he had experienced a vision while singing a hymn from a street pulpit in Edinburgh at the age of seven. Six years later his family emigrated to Australia, where he became a pastor in the Congregational Church. When no organised church could hold him, he became a full-time non-denominational evangelist and faith healer.

He arrived in the USA in 1878, eventually settling at Evanston, Illinois. Here he published a weekly paper decrying everything from doctors to eating pork, and promoting beliefs that the earth was flat and that the Celts were the lost tribe of Israel. In 1896, he established the Christian Catholic Church, which he was at pains to point out had no connection with 'that *other* Catholic church'. Following a decade of legal wrangling with the Chicago authorities, he secretly bought ten square miles of lakefront 40 miles to the north of the city. His goal was to found a true American theocracy.

As clocks struck midnight, chiming in the new century, he announced his plans for Zion. It would be a city of 200,000 inhabitants laid out as a Union Jack. It would have lumber mills and cookie factories, a college, huge auditoria and even its own postage stamp. Settlers were offered 1,100-year leases, 100 years to usher in the Kingdom and 1,000 for Christ's millennial reign. The leases specifically forbade gambling, dancing, swearing, spitting, theatres, circuses, alcohol, tobacco, pork, oysters, doctors, politicians and tan-coloured shoes. Zion was one of the world's earliest communities planned as an integrated city. The first settlers arrived in 1901, about the same time as Dowie hailed himself to be Elijah the Restorer. At the height of his powers, he claimed to be worth several million dollars, thanks to his 50,000 followers, 6,000 of whom lived in Zion City.

Then Dowie's health started to deteriorate. He dressed in priestly robes and enjoyed an increasingly extravagant lifestyle. Rumours of heavy drinking and polygamy started to spread. By 1905 Zion City's 7,500 citizens had deposed their leader. Zion City officially changed its name to Zion in 1919, but for decades it retained many of Dowie's anti-sin statutes. Up to 3,000

Christians throughout the world still describe themselves as 'Dowieites'. Dowie himself has an enduring footnote as a minor tragic character in James Joyce's *Ulysses*.

HONOURING GOD IN FAR-FLUNG PLACES

Religion has unusual ways of travelling the globe. The former Church of Scotland in Dreghorn, Ayrshire, built as a Free Church in 1877, was demolished and shipped out stone by stone to be re-erected as a wedding venue at the Hotel Sunlife Garden, Hiratsuka, in Japan.

A green space in the Taiwanese capital of Taipei, previously known prosaically as Park 18, was renamed the Barclay Memorial Park in 1994. Glaswegian Robert Barclay spent most of his life as a missionary in Tainan, publishing the country's first newspaper and translating the Bible into Taiwanese from 1916 to 1932.

Born in Glasgow in 1841, missionary William Campbell became the first European to visit Sun Moon Lake, Taiwan's largest body of water. He called it Lake Candidius after the seventeenth-century Dutch missionary, although it takes its present name from its topography.

The Mackay Memorial Hospital in Taipei honours not its founder but its benefactor, the widow of a Captain Mackay. Its founder in 1880 was Scots-Canadian missionary George Leslie Mackay, who also established Oxford University College, now the University of Aletheia, in Tamsui. He was the subject of the first-ever Taiwanese opera sung in English, *The Black Bearded Bible Man*, commissioned in 2008.

6

Chance is a fine thing

Being in the right place at the right time played a major part in how hamlets, villages, towns and cities overseas ended up with a Scottish place name. Having responsibility for organising a post office, or supervising the building of a road or railway, or being a civic leader all increased the odds of a person's Scottish name or place of birth being adopted. A landscape feature or view could trigger a burst of homesickness. Some communities changed their name several times, the Scottish version just happening to stick. Thus Broadalbin in New York State started out as Kennyetto, Benedict's Corners and Fonda's Bush before Scottish settlers suggested the variant of the Perthshire district of Breadalbane in 1804. In 1815, the village was officially registered as Rawsonville, after its first doctor, but the name was never used.

Change of name

Place names are surprisingly fluid. It often took several attempts before a settlement finally acquired the name by which it has been known ever since. Sometimes there is no logic as to why a particular name has stuck. The city of Inverness in Citrus County, Florida, started life as Tompkinsville in 1868, when a Confederate veteran, Alfred 'Uncle Alf' Tompkins, bought land on the shores of the Tsala Apopka Lake chain. He sold plots of land or offered them free to would-be settlers. Despite leaving school during sixth grade, fellow settler Francis Dampier laid out the town, opened its first store, became the county's first timber mill owner and tax collector, and ended up serving as county treasurer, mayor, city councillor and police chief.

After the discovery of phosphate nearby, Tompkinsville flourished. A Jacksonville firm agreed to build a new courthouse, if the townspeople agreed to change the name from Tompkinsville to Inverness. Local legend refers to a lonely Scotsman who thought the landscape resembled that of his home town. In 1889, Tompkins sold Tompkinsville to the firm and it became Inverness, selected as the permanent home of justice and local government. In a recent poll, it was discovered that one resident was actually a native of Inverness, Scotland.

Tobermory, Ontario, at the tip of the Bruce Peninsula on Lake Huron, was built around Big Tub Harbour, the deepest natural harbour of the Great Lakes. In 1820 the settlement was known as Collins Harbour before being renamed 'Townplot of Bury' in 1855. Scottish fishermen, however, had called it Tobermory 20 years earlier because it reminded them of Tobermory on Mull. In the longer term, it was Tobermory that was adopted and the two towns are now twinned.

A little bribery helps to change a town's name. The first English settlers named the future Douglas, Massachusetts, New Sherburn in 1715. Dr William Douglas, an eminent Boston physician, renamed it after himself in 1746. In return for the privilege, he offered the inhabitants 30 acres of land and a substantial sum to establish free schools. Born in Haddington and a graduate of Edinburgh University, Douglas was lured to America in 1718 by the prospect of a friend being appointed governor of Massachusetts Bay. Although the appointment fell through, as the only doctor in Boston with a degree Douglas established a substantial and lucrative practice. However, he did not fit well into English Bostonian society because of his race and religion, so looked to buy land at New Sherburn township in Worcester County.

Douglas was typical of the physicians produced by the Scottish Enlightenment. His knowledge and interests extended to botany, history, studying the weather, geography and travel. His foray into political economy earned him the description of the 'honest and downright Dr Douglas' from Adam Smith. He produced the 'mother' or 'type' map that formed the basis of half a century of mapping New England. As a crossroads for stagecoaches, his town attracted stores and inns, as well as the grist and timber mills, which help to earn Douglas's reputation as a heritage town today.

The future city of Calgary, Alberta, traces its roots to a small, wooden fort built in 1875 by the North West Mounted Police at the confluence of the Bow and Elbow rivers. The Canadian government had founded the paramilitary police force two years previously with a view to establishing Canadian sovereignty against the threat of encroachment by the USA, to putting an end to the illicit whiskey trade, and to negotiating with First Nations people in preparation for the treaties that would open up the land for settlement.

At first the fort was simply called 'the Elbow' or 'Bow River Fort' and then briefly Brisebois by Inspector A. E. Brisebois. His superior officers rejected this means of self-promotion. Colonel James MacLeod came up with the suggestion of Calgary after the beach on Mull, near where he had holidayed as a child. Born on the Isle of Skye, at the age of nine MacLeod emigrated with his family to a farm north of Toronto. His training as a lawyer coupled with his love of the outdoor life and respect for the native people of Canada made him an ideal choice as superintendent and inspector in the newly established North West Mounted Police. The arrival of the Canadian Pacific Railway in 1883 put Calgary on the map. By the time it was incorporated as a city 11 years later, the population of 'Sandstone City' had quadrupled, riding on the back of the cattle business. One man's holiday haunt has given rise to a city of over a million people today.

Misspellings

Spelling does not always correctly cross the oceans. For the first 18 months, the now abandoned gold-mining settlement of Rothsay, Western Australia, was correctly spelled after the capital of the island of Bute. However, when the town was registered in 1899, the 'e' was mysteriously dropped, probably as a result of a clerical error.

In 1844, Scotsman Allen Wright named a crossing over the Pecatonica River in Wisconsin after the Duke of Argyll, but he misspelled the name as Argyle. A visiting preacher in 1873 described the village as 'one of the most remarkable Scotch settlements in the United States'.

In the late eighteenth century Mount Sterling, Montgomery County, became the commercial centre for a vast area of newly explored eastern Kentucky. In 1792 Scotsman Hugh Forbes held a land grant for the area adjoining the Little Mountain, a tree-covered 125-foot-high mound which turned out to be an ancient tribal burial site. To speed the town's growth, purchasers of lots from Forbes were required to build a shop or house '16 feet square, of brick, stone, "hugged" logs, or frame' within a year of their arrival. As the settlement grew, the people met to decide on a formal name for the place, which was then called Little Mountain Town. They agreed that Hugh Forbes should choose the new title; he selected Mount Stirling, combining Little Mountain, near which it was established, and Stirling, from his native Scotland. In 1792, the Kentucky Assembly passed an Act establishing the town but incorrectly spelled it Mount Sterling. Four years later, it was chosen to be the county seat. The town achieved its moment of fame in 1864 when the Confederate Army was defeated at the Battle of Mount Sterling.

Wauchope, New South Wales, had its spelling error corrected. Following the establishment of the penal colony at Port Macquarie, stories about the wealth of the large cedar forests in the hinterland attracted the first timber cutters. The area was divided into large estates for retiring British army and naval personnel. Robert Andrew Wauch bought an estate on the King River in 1836. Robert was a descendent of the aristocratic Wauchope family from Edinburgh: his father, however, had dropped the 'ope', owing to a family dispute. After retiring from service in the 28th Regiment of Foot, Wauch emigrated to Sydney with his wife and three children. He bought more property and built Wauch House.

On his death in 1866 the *Government Gazette* published the deeds of his properties, specifying that they should be called Wauchope. Twenty years later a settlement grew up on his estate after the government built a dock to export timber and agricultural products. When the first post office opened in 1882, it was decided to call the new settlement Wauchope. The *Government Gazette* misprinted the name as Wanghope, an error that was corrected seven years later. To confuse matters further, today the name of the town is pronounced War-hope.

David Baldwin Chedester, a wagon-train master from Iowa, was the first settler of the future Livingston, California, in 1862. He supplied provisions to the railroad gangs. One member of a gang, Edward Olds, spotted an opportunity and joined Chedester by opening a saloon and clothing store. The site on the banks of the Merced River grew, as railway construction workers, gold seekers and farmers put down roots and a new town was laid out on each side of the tracks. It was given the name Livingstone after the Scottish-born African explorer David Livingstone whose disappearance at the time was making worldwide headlines. In 1872, however, when petitioning for a new post office, the final 'e' was inadvertently deleted and Livingstone officially became Livingston.

Errors – deliberate or accidental

Other errors can creep in when choosing place names. Sir William Young, the area's first representative in the Assembly at Halifax, suggested the name Inverness, Cape Breton Island, for one of its three administrative districts in 1837. It was assumed that he had chosen the town of his birth until it was discovered that he was actually born in Falkirk.

Young was an ambitious and colourful character – he was also so short in stature that he never lost the nickname 'little Billy Young'. Claiming to have an honours degree from Glasgow University, he emigrated to Nova Scotia with his family in 1814. His aim was to make his fortune as quickly as possible and he soon earned a reputation as a hard-headed merchant. He then switched his career to law. An aspiring lawyer needed to enter politics to succeed and so in 1832 he contested a vacant seat on Cape Breton Island. The first three polling places declared a tie, but, when voting began at the fourth and last station, 150 Scotsmen, armed with clubs, expelled his opponent's friends from the hustings and secured Young's election. The assembly declared the election invalid because of evidence that Young was complicit in the riot; however, in the 1836 election, Young romped home, leading to the new county being named Inverness. There are two explanations as to why it was so-called. Young himself may have lobbied for the name to reflect the Highland character of the local population, or people may have wrongly assumed that Inverness was Young's birthplace.

Brackenridge, Pennsylvania – rather than Breckenridge – is the result not of a spelling mistake but of a deliberate decision. On emigrating with his parents from Ballwilline Farm near Campbeltown in 1753, Hugh Breckenridge changed the family surname to Brackenridge. Hugh later claimed that he altered the spelling 'because I found the bulk of the same stock spelt it so'. Some historians, however, have suggested that, as Hugh was still a child on arrival in the USA, his father may have been responsible for the name change because 'bracken' reminded him of the plant that covered the hillsides of Kintyre.

The family settled in a frontier area of York County which, tellingly, was known as the Barrens. Tradition has it that they had to sell their clothes to finance the journey of nearly 100 miles from their landing point. Hungry for knowledge, young Hugh was prepared to walk 30 miles in order to borrow a book. The learning paid off.

In 1781, Brackenridge set up as a frontier lawyer in the tiny village of Pittsburgh. He became a politician, author and journalist, helping to set up the *Pittsburgh Post Gazette*, the first newspaper west of the Alleghenies. In one article he wrote prophetically: 'This town in future will be a place of great manufactory . . . indeed the greatest on the continent or perhaps in the world.' Thanks to Andrew Carnegie, his prophecy was not far out. Even when appointed an associate justice of the Supreme Court of Pennsylvania, he remained proud of his frontier roots. 'He was not above kicking off his boots while on the bench and delivering his charge to the jury with bare feet propped on the bar of justice.' He was also famous for propping up other bars and becoming involved in brawls.

His son, Col Henry Marie Brackenridge, brought his family in 1827 to the Allegheny Valley, where he built a homestead. This was later demolished to make room for the offices of the Brackenridge Works of the Allegheny Ludlum Steel Corporation. The community decided to honour the Scottish family by naming their town Brackenridge.

Difficult to pronounce

Which Scottish city name is it easiest to pronounce? Aberdeen, Mississippi, started out as Dundee when it was founded in 1834 by Robert Gordon from the parish of Minnigaff in Dumfriesshire. Emigrating in 1810, he joined a group of Native American traders, settling and opening a general store at Cotton Gin Port, then under the control of the formidable Chickasaw tribe. Befriending the local chief, he helped to negotiate the land treaty between the US government and the Chickasaws in 1832.

The presence of the Tombigbee River and the proximity to rich prairie land made the area ideal for cotton growing. Incorporated in 1837, the town initially took the name of Dundee 'after his Scotch home', according to local tradition, but later changed to Aberdeen, or New Aberdeen, because people could not pronounce Dundee. Why he chose Dundee initially remains a mystery, although Aberdeen may have appealed because of its associations with his namesake, Robert Gordon, the famous seventeenth-century Baltic merchant.

By now a wealthy man, Gordon built himself an antebellum-style mansion at nearby Pontotoc, naming it Lochinvar after the ancient home of the Galloway branch of the Gordon family. He employed a Scottish architect and builders, and imported Doric columns from a Scottish castle to support the front porches.

Embellished with grand plantation mansions, the town enjoyed dramatic growth, thanks to 'King Cotton'. By 1850, it was the second-largest city in Mississippi, cotton from the interior being shipped at the port for New Orleans and Mobile. Today, the town's crest incorporates a set of bagpipes. The name Aberdeen continues with Aberdeen Lock and Aberdeen Lake, man-made structures on the Tennessee–Tombigbee Waterway, which serves as a bridge between the Tennessee River and the Gulf of Mexico.

Adding a Scottish flavour

Although many Scottish place names have been lost in the drive to restore aboriginal names, Wingatui, New Zealand, is a Scottish original. Despite having a Maori ring to it, it simply shows the fondness of Scottish settlers for novel names. It is mock Maori, meaning 'to wing [shoot and injure] a tui bird'. The name stirred up a fierce debate in the *Otago Times* in the 1890s, with some protagonists arguing that it was a corruption of the Maori, 'the place for waiting of the spirits', while others supported the view that a Mr Stevenson named it as a reference to his skills as a marksman. Now a suburb of Mosgiel near Dunedin, Wingatui was an important railway junction, taking agricultural produce to the cities and crowds to the local racecourse. Glentui, near Canterbury, has an even stronger Scottish twist, although there is no obvious connection. Londoner H. C. H. Knowles opened a sheep station in the Tui Valley in 1854, perhaps adding 'Glen' because it reminded him of Scotland – or simply because prefixing names with 'Glen' was very fashionable at the time.

Avoiding confusion

The former mining town of Grampian, Clearfield County, Pennsylvania, was incorporated as Pennville in 1885 but, owing to confusion with the similarly named Penfield, its name was changed to Grampian a decade later. The town lies among what are known as the 'Grampian Hills', named by early settler Dr Samuel Coleman due to their resemblance to the Grampians in north-east Scotland. Although Coleman had migrated here from East Pennsylvania in 1809, his parents were Scottish and indeed he claimed noble blood. Nearby settlements such as Hepburnia, Ferguson and Stronach reinforce the Scottish connection.

Edinburgh, Edinburg or Edinboro? Settlers on the shores of the Great Sacandaga Lake, New York State, arrived from 1787. Some had first encountered the area, with its fertile land and virgin pine forests, when serving in the American Revolutionary Wars. In 1801, the settlers decided that the community was big enough to merit its own name and chose Northfield. Seven years later it was renamed Edinburgh after the discovery was made of another Northfield in New York State. Farming, logging and timber products became the mainstays of the economy of the town, which was also known as Edinburg or Edinboro. In the early 1930s, however, it vanished from the map under the waters of the newly created Sacandaga Reservoir.

Post office towns

A landmark in the history of many settlements was the day when the post office opened. In order to achieve this, the settlement needed a name. By the 1880s, the future Abernethy, Saskatchewan, was large enough to merit a post office to sort and deliver the seed catalogues and letters from home. Based at nearby

Indian Head, Scottish merchant Robert Balcarres Crawford was in charge of appointments to post offices and mail carriers. He organised a mail run from Balcarres, which he labelled using his own middle name, to Abernethy, which he named after the street where he had been brought up in Glasgow. Like so many pioneer towns, Abernethy and Balcarres grew because they were stops on the Canadian Pacific Railway. After a long and hard-fought campaign by local settlers, the first CPR train rolled across the Trestle Bridge over Pheasant Creek in 1904. Abernethy still hosts one of the longest-running agricultural fairs in the province.

On the south-east shore of Lake Nipissing, Callander, Ontario, shares attributes with its Scottish cousin in the Trossachs. Both are holiday resorts set among mountains and forests, with fishing as a major sport. The Canadian Callander owes its roots to intrepid pioneers George Morrison and his wife Elizabeth, who travelled by raft and corduroy roads, made of logs placed side by side, to set up their homestead. Elizabeth was the first white woman in the area. George opened a general store and in 1881 a post office in the expectation that the railway would soon reach the town: it arrived five years later. Morrison named the town Callander after his parents' birthplace. It took some time, however, for the new name to stick, some locals referring to it as South East Shore for many years. In 1934 Callander gained a new industry – tourism – after the birth of the Dionne quintuplets, the world's first known quins to survive infancy. Because of the quins, Callander became a greater Canadian tourist attraction than the Niagara Falls, with film stars such as Bette Davis and James Cagney coming to pay their respects.

The story of Bon Accord, Alberta, starts with the French Oblates of the St Albert Catholic Mission, who established timber and flour mills on the south bank of the Sturgeon River in 1878. Although fire destroyed the mills a decade later, by then settlers were moving into the area. In 1896 eight settlers, including Sandy Florence from Aberdeen, met to set up an official school district. They chose the name Bon Accord, supposedly the watchword used by supporters of Robert the Bruce when the English occupied Aberdeen Castle in 1307. They also adopted the name for the post office and the village. When the railroad announced that it was setting up a new town a mile east of Bon Accord, the citizens decided to move, taking the name with them. Today, the commuter town, 25 miles north of Edmonton, translates the motto as: 'Happy to meet, sorry to part, happy to meet again.'

Named by chance

John Pitcairn from Dysart in Fife earned his place in the history books for being in charge of the British troops at Lexington in 1775 when the rebels fired the first shots of the American Revolutionary Wars. His horse was shot from under him, but he survived. Two months later he died a hero's death at the Battle of Bunker Hill.

The name of his son Robert features in world atlases. He discovered the Pitcairn Islands, the remote Pacific outposts lying halfway between New Zealand and South America. In 1766, the 14-year-old midshipman joined the crew of HMS *Swallow* under the command of Captain Philip Carteret on a round-the-world voyage of exploration. The *Swallow*'s log for 2 July 1767 records Robert's discovery: 'It is so high that we saw it at a distance of more than fifteen leagues, and it having been discovered by a young gentleman, son to Major Pitcairn of the marines, we called it Pitcairn's Island.' The weather, however, was too stormy to land. Robert never knew how famous his island was to become when, 40 years later, nine of the crew who had mutinied on the *Bounty* became its first inhabitants. Two years after discovering Pitcairn he sailed on HMS *Aurora* from the Cape of Good Hope headed for India. The ship and her crew were never heard of again.

More than one story

There are at least two explanations as to how Inverness, Stockholm, acquired its name. One is that Scottish mercenaries fighting in the Swedish army during the seventeenth century were barracked there, sufficiently far away from central Stockholm so they would not disturb the peace. The other is that a Swede had visited Scotland on his Grand Tour and liked the Inverness area so much that he named his country estate after it.

Sometimes people's imagination simply dried up when having to come up with the name for railway stations. Ohai in Southland, New Zealand, may be a case in point. Officially, the town takes its name from the Maori 'place of the stone', which some authorities believe was in use prior to the 1840s. There is, however, a more colourful version of the story. In the 1920s Scotsman Alexander Wylie Rodger owned the Birchwood sheep station, as well as having interests in coal-mining, butter manufacture and railways. When approached to name a station on his land, he prevaricated so long that the railway agent lost patience and asked 'Have you thought of a name yet?' to which Mr Rodger replied 'Oh aye.' And so, Ohai it was. What the name was that Mr Rodger had in mind was never divulged.

Edinburgh was the first settlement in Johnson County, Indiana. Its first resident, John Campbell, arrived in 1820. How Edinburgh acquired its name is unclear. Some accounts say that one early landowner was Scotsman Alexander Thompson, while others suggest that he was born in Virginia of Scottish-Irish parentage. Another account claims that early settlers knew the area as Eden because of its natural beauty and so Edinburgh was adopted over time. After the arrival of the railroad in 1845, the town's population doubled, and Edinburgh became the leading grain and pork market in central Indiana and the county's industrial hub. Why Edinburgh dropped the 'h' from its name from 1899 to 1977, when the town council restored it, is a mystery, just like the origin of its name. There was a general trend in the USA to adopt the German 'burg' rather than the Scots 'burgh' or the English 'borough', which may account for the change in spelling.

It's my town

Hamilton, Ontario's fourth-largest city, was named by private town promoter George Hamilton. His father, Robert Hamilton, born in Bolton, East Lothian, moved to Canada to work for a fur-trading company. In 1780, he went into business as supplier and haulier to the British Army at Fort Niagara, as well as acquiring extensive landholdings on the Niagara peninsula. Robert sent his son George back to Edinburgh in 1795 to be educated. On his return, George inherited his father's business interests until the War of 1812 intervened.

Hamilton's house was burned down by billeted British troops and his business failed. Hearing of plans to create a new administrative centre at the 'Head of the Lake' (Hamilton Harbour), Hamilton shrewdly purchased land in the area on which a court-house and jail were built. He laid out the town in the standard grid pattern adopted in most of Upper Canada and naturally named it after himself. As a representative in the Legislative Assembly of Upper Canada from 1821 to 1830, he actively encouraged emigration from the old country to the young country.

Two bites at the cherry

Edinburg and Edina, Missouri – this tale of two cities and two names has one author, attorney Stephen Carnegy, whose roots lay in Scotland's capital. He established Edinburg in 1836 after 'two old bachelors' opened a grocery store, relying largely on the sale of spirits in the hamlet then known as Buck Snort. In 1839, Carnegy surveyed the land for a second town – on high ground with a source of water and views over gently rolling hills. Again, he reverted to his ancestral city, adopting the name Edina, made fashionable by Robert Burns. Edina was incorporated as a city in 1851 and is now the capital of Knox County.

Incorporated in 1924, Dundee was built on the wealth of Florida's citrus industry. In 1910, one of the first settlers, Mr Menzie from Dundee, decreed that the tiny settlement should be called after his former home. He also named one of Dundee's many lakes, Lake Menzie. The following year a branch of the Atlantic Coast Line Railroad arrived in Dundee, and land speculators and developers soon followed. One of the first was the Highlands Development Co., who ran special trains, refunding the rail fare of any potential settler who bought land. To accommodate the influx of people, a large tent was erected near the station until the Highlands Hotel could be built. The Scottish theme continued with the Glen St Mary Nursery Company, who created 900 acres of citrus orchards.

A matter of dispute

The Scots and Irish battle over Fingal, New South Wales. Fingal Head and the small beach community of Fingal lie at the mouth of the Tweed River. When Captain Cook was nearly shipwrecked here, he chose to name the two landmarks Mount

Warning and Point Danger. After a lighthouse was built at Fingal Head in the 1870s, locals nicknamed the offshore outcrop of columnar-jointed basalt 'the Giant's Causeway'. Fingal was the legendary giant whose causeway linked Northern Ireland's Antrim coast with the island of Staffa. Both Irish and Scottish settlers claimed the origin of the name of Fingal for themselves.

The naming of Edina, Minnesota, has been a source of community debate for decades. The story goes that when it became a village in 1888 the Scottish and Irish communities argued as to whether to call it Killarney or Edina; however, recent research by local historians has revealed a different story. There were only two Scots living in the village in 1888, the rival communities being Irish and Americans from the East Coast. In 1869 Andrew Craik from Edinburgh had bought a mill, which he renamed Edina Mill. At the three meetings held to resolve the village's name, Craik supported Edina, the name proposed by a neighbouring farmer. The minutes of the first meeting record: 'Motion made and seconded the village be called "Hennepin Park". Carried. Motion made and seconded to reconsider the motion just taken. Carried. Moved and seconded that the village be called "Westfield". Carried. Moved and carried to adjourn.' The second meeting was 'somewhat boisterous', with several committee members resigning. At the third meeting, Edina finally won the day, with 47 for and 42 against.

Despite marketing itself as 'a wee bit of Ireland in the heart of the Ottawa Valley . . . where leprechauns make their home and the luck of the Irish abounds', Douglas, Ontario, is more Scots than Irish. In 1853, Judge John G. Malloch bought land and had it surveyed for a village, which he named Douglas. Malloch was one of the members of the 'Perth Military Colony', a body of soldiers who, having been honourably discharged from military service, were sent in to take up land in Lanark County in 1816.

Many spent the first summer living in tents or bark huts until the trees could be felled for log cabins. Douglas is now famous for its annual St Patrick's Day parade.

Water has always been the lifeblood of Dunedin, Pinellas County, Florida, now a beach resort on the Gulf of Mexico. Many early residents were boating enthusiasts, which was just as well: the only way to reach Dunedin was by water or horseback. After John L. Branch, proprietor of the settlement's first store, built a dock around 1870, the community became the trading centre for the area. Two Scots, J. O. Douglas and James Somerville from Edinburgh, built a general store on the waterfront, and George L. Jones from Georgia opened a rival store opposite. Jones put up a sign – 'Jonesboro' – outside his store and, not to be outdone, Douglas and Somerville soon had a sign swinging over their doorway too, theirs reading 'Dunedin'. The settlers preferred the name Dunedin and so the Scots petitioned the federal government for a post office to be called the same. The town was officially designated Dunedin in 1899. Dunedin is very proud of its Scottish connections, choosing Stirling as its sister city and naming its golf course Dunedin Stirling Links. The annual Highland Games features musical contributions from the Scottish Highlander Band, and the City of Dunedin Pipe and Drum Corps.

A matter of chance

Although the first homesteaders from the 1880s onwards were predominantly Irish, it was a Scot who was behind the naming of the city of Clyde Hill, Washington State. Regular commuters on the Yarrow Point to Seattle ferry, most of whom were of Irish descent, had passed the time giving unofficial Irish names to nearby roads. The trip to the boat landing reminded one commuter of his home on the Firth of Clyde. He suggested Clyde Road, which by 1947 was the town's main thoroughfare. The future city was expanding and a Community Club was formed, its first task being to decide on a name. Although the neighbouring Bellevue post office delivered the mail to the area, the club felt that a distinct community deserved a distinct name. Six years later, in 1953, the city of Clyde Hill was officially incorporated.

Winning the lottery is one way to name a town. Dundee, Illinois, is a town of two halves, East and West Dundee, separated by the Fox River. In 1835, the Oatmans opened a tavern and store that became the core of the township of European settlers. Two years later they held a lottery to decide who would name the town. The winner was Alexander Gardiner, who chose Dundee in honour of his home town. Six years later another emigrant Scot, this time from Glasgow, set up shop as a cooper, a far cry from his later enterprise as founder of the legendary Pinkerton Detective Agency.

The two halves of Dundee developed very differently. While West Dundee's prosperity was based on a tree nursery founded in 1855, East Dundee took a more industrial path, with flourishing brickworks using clay from the river and employing workers from the largely Lutheran German community. Relations between them and the largely Scottish community of West Dundee were not always cordial.

Mistaken identity

Mount Glasgow, Alberta, was named after a battleship rather than Scotland's largest city. The distinctive, pyramid-shaped mountain, rising 9,630 feet in the Canadian Rockies, was named in 1922 after the 4,800-ton battleship HMS *Glasgow*. Launched from Fairfield's Govan shipyard in 1909, she helped to sink a

German cruiser and scuttle another during the Battle of the Falklands in 1914. Members of the Alberta–British Columbia boundary survey of 1913–25 named many of the features of the area. At a time when postwar patriotism was at its height, they chose to honour warships, French villages, war heroes, songs of the era, generals, admirals and little-known soldiers who had left the survey to die in the trenches.

SOUNDS SCOTTISH

Contrary to many listings of Scottish place names, not all that seem Scottish actually have Scottish associations. The origin of some names has been lost over time; often if they sound Scottish or use a surname prevalent in Scotland, they are assumed, rightly or wrongly, to have been named by or after Scots. Names prefixed with Mc or Mac may have Irish as well as Scottish origins.

Morningside does not refer exclusively to the suburb of Edinburgh but was a popular choice for any location built on the side of a hill that caught the early sun. There are Morningsides in Canada, the USA, South Africa, Australia and New Zealand.

Kelso, California, was named after not the Scottish Borders town but a railroad worker, John Kelso, whose name was put in a hat alongside two other workers' in order to decide the name of Siding 16 on the new railway between Utah and Los Angeles in 1905.

The ghost town of Alva, Wyoming, was named not after the Clackmannanshire town but after Alva S. Bender, the first postmaster.

Elgin, North Dakota, was originally Shanley until it became confused with Stanley, another station on the new railway line. A group of passengers passed the time while waiting for a train by discussing possible names. One passenger looked at his watch and suggested Elgin, the brand name of a famous watchmaker.

Abbotsford, Wisconsin, and Abbotsford, New Zealand, were named after a Mr Abbots rather than by Sir Walter Scott readers.

Annandale, a district of the Indian hill station Shimla, was christened by one of the first settlers, Captain Charles Pratt Kennedy. He was so struck by the beauty of the valley that he named it Annadale, after Anna, a sweetheart of his youth. Over time the spelling changed to Annandale.

Although a Free Church of Scotland mission station, Blythswood, South Africa, honoured Captain Matthew Blyth, a representative of the Cape Colony government.

Calabogie, Ontario, most likely originated in the native name for a sturgeon, although some authorities claim it comes from the Gaelic '*calladh bogaidh*', meaning a marshy bay.

Coronach, Saskatchewan, was named after a famous racehorse. It won the Derby in 1926, the same year as the Canadian Pacific Railway started building the railroad settlement. A *coronach* in Scottish and Irish Gaelic is a funeral lament. Similarly, gold diggers named Marvel Loch in Western Australia after a winning racehorse.

There are several theories as to how Dallas in Texas was given its name, but none relate to the village of Dallas in Moray.

Fort Ross, California, derives not from the Scottish clan but from a poetic name for Russia. The Russian-American Company opened the trading base to supply Alaska in 1812.

The 'Helen' of Helensburgh, New South Wales, was the daughter of the local mine promoter, in the same way as Helensburgh on the Clyde took its name from the wife of the town's late eighteenth-century founder, Sir James Colquhoun.

Napier, New Zealand, is called after the military leader General Sir Charles Napier who, although of Scottish ancestry, was born in the Palace of Whitehall, London.

Nevis in the Caribbean was originally Santa Maria de las Nieves – Our Lady of the Snows. The name was shortened to Nieves and anglicised by the British to Nevis.

Despite all the Scottish names within the region of South Island, New Zealand, Otago was adopted from an old Maori name, possibly meaning 'the place of red earth'.

7

Honouring heroes

Overseas place names often reflect Scottish heroes, from distinguished scientists to poets. They also give a nod to colonial governors and politicians, with perhaps an element of flattery and forelock tugging involved. Literary figures and military men also earn a place in the pantheon of Scottish place names.

The Scientists

Scotland has always punched above its weight in the field of scientific endeavour. In the naming of landscapes and settlements, the geologists have been particularly favoured, perhaps because explorers and surveyors had particular respect for the men who understood how the land was formed.

Whaler's son and explorer William Scoresby from Whitby named Jameson Land in eastern Greenland after his lifelong friend, teacher and geologist, Robert Jameson.

Born in Leith in 1774, as a young man Jameson was dissuaded from going to sea. In 1803, he took over the chair of natural history at Edinburgh University, a post he held with distinction for the rest of his life. Charles Darwin was among his students.

In 1806, Scoresby enrolled at Edinburgh University after a summer spent with his father, master of the *Resolution*. During the trip they took their ship to a record northing, reaching

81° 30'. Young Scoresby spent the winters studying chemistry and natural philosophy. He was keen to learn about polar seas and his teachers urged him to carry out research during his Arctic summers.

Between 1813 and 1817 Scoresby sailed to the Arctic in command of the *Esk*, making many of his most important discoveries in Arctic geography, meteorology and oceanography. In 1819, he was elected a fellow of the Royal Society of Edinburgh, one of his sponsors being Robert Jameson. Three years later he charted and named a large section of the east coast of Greenland, not learning until he returned of his wife's death. He made one last voyage before he entered the Church. Scoresby honoured several other Scottish scientists and friends, including the pioneer of optics, David Brewster, at Cape Brewster, and the moral philosopher Dugald Stewart at Cape Stewart. David Brewster is also celebrated at the other end of the globe, in New Zealand's Southern Alps, by Mount Brewster and the Brewster Glacier.

South Island may represent the world's greatest concentration of scientists' names on the map. When surveying these wilderness areas, the German-born explorer Julius von Haast named more than a hundred mountain peaks and other features after famous scientists. In 1862, he wrote: 'I proposed myself to create a kind of Pantheon or Walhalla for my illustrious contemporaries amongst those never-trodden peaks and glaciers.'

Given that his task was naming landscape features, it is not surprising that von Haast leaned towards geologists. For example, he honoured Sir Charles Lyell, who popularised James Hutton's theory of the evolution of the Earth, with Mount Lyell. Incidentally, Lyell was generally a popular choice, with the Lyell Glacier in the Sierra Nevada Mountains; Mount Lyell, the highest peak in Yosemite National Park, California; Lyell, described as New Zealand's most inaccessible gold-mining town; and Mount Lyell, Tasmania.

Von Haast acknowledged James Hutton himself, 'the father of geology', in Mount Hutton and another populariser of Hutton's theories, John Playfair, in Mount Playfair. He awarded Sir Roderick Impey Murchison, the geologist who may have first predicted the presence of gold in Australia, Mount Impey and Mount Murchison, as well as the River Murchison. James Forbes, the glaciologist, was not forgotten, with the Forbes River and a Mount Forbes; nor was Andrew Crombie Ramsay, who served the British Geological Survey for 40 years, his name being remembered in the Ramsay Glacier and Mount Ramsay.

Von Haast did not forget friends either. Scottish doctor Andrew Sinclair was the Colonial Secretary of New Zealand from 1844 to 1856. A keen botanist, in his retirement he joined von Haast in plant collecting expeditions until he drowned in the Rangitata River in 1861. Von Haast remembered him by Mount Sinclair, the Sinclair Range and Sinclair River.

Glasgow University graduate James McKerrow continued von Haast's precedent of naming land features after scientists. He explored the Otago Lakes district in New Zealand as a land surveyor. Geologists James Forbes and Roderick Murchison collected their second mountains in Mount Murchison and Mount Forbes. He awarded geologist and writer Hugh Miller his first mountain in the Miller Peak.

Another of McKerrow's heroes was David Lyall, the botanist and explorer, whose name he commemorated in Mount Lyall on Campbell Island, New Zealand. Born in 1817 in Auchenblae, Kincardineshire, Lyall served as ship's surgeon on a Greenland whaler before joining the navy as assistant surgeon on Captain James Clark Ross's scientific expedition to the Antarctic in 1839. He made two visits to Campbell Island, observing the wildlife and collecting more than 1,500 plant species. One contemporary remarked, 'tho' not a very talkative man, we get curious yarns from him at times'. David Lyall is also remembered in Lyall Bay, now a seaside suburb of Wellington, New Zealand, and the Lyall Islands in Victoria Land, Antarctica.

In 1860 von Haast had named the main features of the Paparoa Range on New Zealand's West Coast. As surveyors further investigated the area, they kept to von Haast's theme, from Euclid to Einstein. Scots honoured by mountain peaks include Alexander Fleming, who discovered penicillin (Mount Fleming); Nobel Laureate William Ramsay, who identified 'the noble gases' (Mount Ramsay); James Dewar, inventor of the Thermos flask (Mount Dewar); and the giant of nineteenth-century physics, Lord Kelvin (Mount Kelvin).

Holding a post such as Director General of the British Geological Survey helped individuals to earn immortality. Born in Muir of Ord, Easter Ross, Sir Roderick Impey Murchison was the second incumbent of the post from 1845. As well as being recognised both by von Haast and McKerrow, he was celebrated by English explorer Samuel Baker in the Murchison Falls on the Nile in Uganda. Despite his prediction about gold in Australia, Murchison, Victoria, is not named not after him but a relative, Captain John Murchison.

Roderick's relative John Murchison seems to have travelled the globe, marrying in Nova Scotia in 1826 and fathering at least one child in the West Indies before settling as a farmer at the Flowerdale Station at Kerrisdale, Victoria. A township was established on the Goulburn River in 1854 and named Murchison in his honour. By now the first vineyards were being established and the village ran a ferry service, punting gold miners across the river.

Sir Roderick donated money to found the first chair of geology at Edinburgh University. Edinburgh-born Archibald Geikie was the first professor and later the director of the British

Geological Survey from 1882 to 1901. Although he visited few, if any, of the places named after him, he is remembered in the Geikie River, Saskatchewan, in northern Canada; the Geikie Glacier on South Georgia; and the Geikie Gorge and mountain range in Western Australia.

One of Scotland's most remarkable all-rounders, Hugh Miller, was born in Cromarty. His seafaring father died when he was just five. Hugh spent 17 years as a jobbing stonemason, acquiring skills which stood him in good stead when investigating the fossils and rock features of what he later called the Old Red Sandstone. His passionate embracing of the need for Church reform led to his move to Edinburgh in 1849 as editor of *The Witness*, the voice of the Free Church of Scotland. Nearly six foot tall, and with a shock of flaming red hair, Miller became a well-known sight in the city streets. Entirely self-taught, his discoveries of Devonian fossil fish and his talents as a writer popularising the theory of evolution raised him to the front rank of natural scientists.

In the same year as Miller moved to Edinburgh, Canadian geologist Abraham Gesner was finding Devonian plant and fish fossils at Escuminac Bay along the southern shore of the Gaspé Peninsula in Quebec. The provincial government designated the area, which became a World Heritage Site in 1999, the Hugh Miller Cliffs in honour of the Scottish geologist. The Hugh Miller Glacier and Hugh Miller Inlet in Alaska were named by fellow Scot John Muir from Dunbar, who shared Miller's curiosity, love of the natural world and ability to describe landscape. Muir discovered the glacier during his travels in Alaska in 1879: 'an imposing array of jagged spires and pyramids, and flat-topped towers and battlements, of many shades of blue, from pale, shimmering, limpid tones in the crevasses and hollows, to the most startling, chilling, almost shrieking vitriol blue on the plain mural spaces from which bergs had just been discharged'. Muir himself was later remembered by the Muir Glacier and Inlet, Alaska.

Although revered throughout the United States in the names of streets, schools, nature trails and even tearooms as founder of the national parks movement, Muir has scarcely left his name on the wild places that he so loved. He did, however, name Mount Emerson in the Sierra Nevada after his friend, the American writer Ralph Waldo Emerson, who visited the Yosemite Valley with him in 1871. Although 'the colossal silver firs, Douglas spruce, *Libocedrus* and sugar pine, the kings and priests of the conifers of the earth, filled him with awe and delight', Emerson declined Muir's invitation to camp under the stars, preferring the comfort of his hotel.

Engineers have proved less likely candidates to win a listing in the index of the world atlas. One exception is Thomas Telford. He is commemorated in Telford New Town in Shropshire, which is also unusual as few place names in other parts of the UK have Scottish roots. Telford officially took its name five years after designation in 1963, when originally it was going to be called Dawley New Town after one of the existing communities that it encompassed. It was then decided to honour the eighteenth-century Scottish road and canal builder and surveyor for the county of Shropshire. Telford is often described as 'the father of civil engineering'.

Why the small town of Telford, Pennsylvania, chose to call itself after the famous Scottish engineer is more obscure. Around 40 miles north-west of Philadelphia, it grew up to service the surrounding agricultural community. Initially it was called Hendrick's Blacksmith, and then County Line, as it straddled two counties. In 1857, when the new railroad cut through the village, the railway company decided to name its station Telford. Today, it is one of the Classic Towns of Greater Philadelphia.

Royalty

Albany, New York, is an early example of a place name honouring royalty. At the time the fur-trading post was known by the Dutch name Beverwyck. When the Dutch surrendered to the British in 1664, King Charles II granted their territory, including New Netherland, New England, Long Island and Delaware, to his brother, the future King James II. New Amsterdam became New York after the royal title Duke of York, and Beverwyck adopted James's Scottish title, Duke of Albany. The name later gained popularity, with 16 Albanys worldwide. The proposal to adopt Albania as the name for the area west of the Hudson River was short-lived, it being renamed New Jersey with the duke's approval.

In the nineteenth century many place names of Empire acknowledged their Queen and her sons and daughters. From the Australian states of Victoria and Queensland to mountain peaks and deserts, dozens of cities, towns and landscape features paid homage to their Queen, not to mention hundreds of streets, parks and public institutions. When the future federal dominion of Canada was under discussion, Victorialia was one of the names considered.

Scots loyally made their contribution to this cause: Orcadian explorer John Rae named Prince of Wales Island, now Wales Island, in the Canadian Arctic, while colonial administrator Sir William McGregor from Towie, Aberdeenshire, climbed 'the Great Mountain' in Papua New Guinea and renamed it Mount Victoria.

A royal visit proved perfectly timed for the small community of Rothesay, New Brunswick. For some years, there had been debate among the locals as to what to call the nameless settlements along the Kennebecasis River, with supporters for

Scribner's Corner, Drury's, Nine-Mile Station and Kennebecasis Bay. The impending visit of young Edward, Prince of Wales in 1860 ended the argument. Aged only 19, Queen Victoria's son, whose Scottish title was Duke of Rothesay, was the first member of the British royal family to visit North America. He left the train at Rothesay, having arrived from nearby St John, where he had arrived on HMS *Styx* a few days earlier. He then continued his journey to Fredericton by ship. Some local historians push the connection with Rothesay on Bute even further, arguing that the Prince himself suggested the name because he liked it. The Kennebecasis railway station where he dismounted was also renamed Rothesay.

Regina, Saskatchewan, has a closer royal connection. Situated almost in the centre of North America, it was a flat feature-less plain hunted over by the First Nation people until the early 1880s, when European settlers arrived. A village called Pile of Bones sprang up, thanks to the fertility and cheapness of the land. Under the Dominion Lands Act, new homesteaders could claim 160 acres of land for just $10. In 1882 it was felt that such a name was unfitting for a town with ambitions. Princess Louise suggested the name Regina, the Latin for Queen. The princess was Queen Victoria's fourth daughter and the wife of John Campbell, Marquess of Lorne and future 9th Duke of Argyll, who served as Governor-General of Canada from 1878 to 1883. Victoria as a name had already been taken for the capital of British Columbia, so the inhabitants settled for Regina.

With a current population of over 200,000, Regina may have had a royal name in 1882 but it had a fair way to go before achieving city status. Settlers camped in tents or small shacks, despite temperatures of minus 40 degrees Centigrade in winter and over 40 degrees in summer. There were neither roads nor pavements, and livestock roamed the streets. Nonetheless, the small town grew and grew. This was helped by the decision to move the headquarters of the North West Mounted Police to Regina and to declare it capital of the Northwest Territories, a land mass larger than the whole of Europe. By 1900 the population was close to 3,000 and six years later Regina was declared capital of the new and fastest-growing Canadian province of Saskatchewan. Princess Louise herself was also remembered in Lake Louise, Alberta, and the hamlet of the same name, which was originally called Laggan.

Edinburgh of the Seven Seas, Tristan da Cunha, is the world's most remote human settlement, being 1,500 miles from its nearest neighbour, St Helena. Both are part of the British Overseas Territories. Discovered and named by the Portuguese in 1506, Tristan was a stopping-off point for shipping between Britain and India. Few attempts to establish a trading post, however, were made until a British garrison took possession in 1816, briefly creating Fort Malcolm as a base. The government was concerned about possible attempts by the French to rescue Napoleon, held as a prisoner on St Helena, and the risk of the island falling into American hands. When the base was abandoned a year later, a small group persuaded the British government to allow them to remain. The commander of the ship that took off the troops presented them with a bull, a cow and few sheep, which in time became an extensive herd and flock.

The leader of the group was Corporal William Glass, accompanied by his South African wife and two children. Born William Glasgow in Kelso in 1786, he changed his name to Glass after enlisting in the army. Under Glass, the group began a remarkable project, which they called 'the Firm', each member signing voluntary agreement of communal living. As well as producing 16 children, Glass ruled the community in patriarchal fashion, reading daily morning and evening prayers to the islanders. Residents came and went, including shipwrecked passengers and crew. The long-term future of the community was established only when five female volunteers from St Helena agreed to join the lonely men. Increasing whaling activity in the area brought new blood.

The death of William Glass in 1853 and the departure of the pastor four years later resulted in an exodus, with only four families remaining on the increasingly isolated outpost. Seagoing traffic fell with the American Civil War, the opening of the Suez Canal and the switch from sail to steam. One ship that did call in, in 1867, was HMS *Galatea*, carrying a very distinguished passenger, HRH Alfred, Duke of Edinburgh and second son of Queen Victoria. In his honour the Settlement, as it is still known, officially became Edinburgh of the Seven Seas. Today, over 250 people live on Tristan, where Glass's principles still hold true. All land is communally owned and stock numbers are controlled to conserve grass and to avoid some families becoming richer than others.

Other royal associations were also popular. Rush's Platform on the Picton–Mittagong loop railway in New South Wales was renamed Braemar in 1892 when the railway company marketed the area as 'the choicest position for summer residence'. The name honours Queen Victoria's holiday retreat. Like its Scottish namesake, the area round Braemar, NSW, is known as the Southern Highlands.

Entrepreneur Donald Smith chose to honour a line of early Scottish kings rather than his monarch, naming a railway station on the Alberta stretch of the Canadian Pacific Railway Canmore in 1884. The name recalled King Malcolm III, husband of the future Saint Margaret. Two years later Queen Victoria granted the settlement a mining licence and the town boomed. When the mines closed in 1979, it looked as if Canmore would join the list of Canada's ghost towns. However, it was then announced that nearby Calgary was to host the 1998 Winter Olympics and Canmore was identified as the host for Nordic cross-country skiing events. Today, the problem is containing the burgeoning population of the mountain resort.

Politicians and colonial administrators

Whether to curry favour, pay their genuine respects or because of a shortage of ideas, many communities chose to name their settlements after colonial governors and administrators or after politicians who had at most a distant association with the area. For example, the popularity of the place name Aberdeen in Canada is attributed to John Campbell Hamilton-Gordon, 1st Marquess of Aberdeen and the seventh Governor-General of Canada, from 1893 to 1898. There have been some more un-usual reasons, however, for honouring the 'great and the good', although colonial governors have been particularly vulnerable to the modern movement in India, Australia and much of Africa where aboriginal names have been reinstated.

The Aberdeen family had fingers in the pies of many con-tinents. Aberdeen Harbour, Hong Kong, is the original Hong Kong – Heung Kong, the 'fragrant harbour' – which traded in incense trees. Early nineteenth-century British merchants in silk, tea, spices and opium who landed near Aberdeen assumed that the name Hong Kong referred to the whole island. So a new name was needed for the harbour area. In 1845, three years after the Chinese ceded the island to Britain, the area was named Aberdeen in honour of the Foreign Secretary and future Prime Minister, George Hamilton-Gordon, 4th Earl of Aberdeen.

The 4th Earl may also have given his name to Aberdeen Island, Sierra Leone, the wealthy beach resort that connects the capital Freetown with its international airport. As Foreign Secretary in the Peel administration of 1841–46, he received reports from the Commissioners of Sierra Leone on progress towards the emancipation of slaves. Another theory is that Aberdeen may refer to the captain of a ship carrying freed slaves back to Africa after the foundation of Freetown in 1787.

As Governor-General of Canada, the 1st Marquess of Aberdeen and his wife, Ishbel, were popular and sociable, and were regular visitors to their far-flung territory. They liked to refer to themselves as 'we twa'. Ishbel took an active interest in Canadian affairs and, struck by the isolated lifestyle of many pioneers, founded the Aberdeen Association for Distribution of Good Literature to Settlers in the West. Aberdeen, Cape Breton Island, on the banks of the Bras d'Or Lakes, was originally simply known as North Side, Whycocomagh Bay. It was a farming community of emigrants largely from Tiree, North Uist, Lewis, Harris and Skye, settled from the 1820s onwards. The area developed as a resort, owing to its scenery and the spa of Salt Mountain, and it is thought that residents changed the name to Aberdeen after the Marquis and his wife stayed at the local Bayview Hotel while taking the waters in the 1890s. The hotel was run by Thomas Mitchell: 'a cheerful and canny Scot, knows how to cook and carve, and is withal a good deal of a wit and a wag . . . Tom will not only satisfy the stomach, but will also elevate the soul.'

An accident of Lady Aberdeen's gave rise to Aberdeen Bridge, Ontario, the first upstream crossing of the Gatineau, a tributary of the Ottawa River. After falling through the ice on her way back from a meeting at a nearby church, Ishbel was rescued by Gatineau locals, who christened the bridge in her honour in 1896.

Canada also honoured its local MPs. Angus, Ontario, was originally called Pine River when laid out around 1855 by Jonas Tarbrush. Twenty years earlier, there had been plans for a village to be named Rippon, but these remained on paper. By now, however, there were roads and a timber mill, the attraction being the magnificent stands of virgin pine to be turned into masts and spars for the Royal Navy. The arrival of the railway stimulated development further and Tarbrush decided to name the new town Angus after Angus Morrison, the first MP for the area. Born in Edinburgh in 1822, Morrison had come to Upper Canada with his father, Hugh, who opened the Golden Ball Tavern in York, Toronto. Although a Toronto-based lawyer, Angus won the election for the newly created district of Simcoe North, his popularity being based on his promotion of transport links. His tenure was relatively short-lived. He lost the 1863 election despite the report that 'Whiskey was sent into the Townships in streams.' Angus's town, however, thrived as the transport hub for 29 sawmills until the pines were exhausted.

Governors of individual provinces also fared well in Canada. Henry Dundas, 1st Viscount Melville, never visited Canada, much less Dundas, Ontario, now part of the city of Hamilton, despite fiercely preserving its separate identity. Henry Dundas, nicknamed King Harry the Ninth because of his control of politics, was a close friend of John Graves Simcoe, Lieutenant Governor of Upper Canada. Simcoe changed the name of the town, laid out in 1797, from Coote's Paradise to the more official-sounding Dundas.

Dundas was once the terminus of Toronto's Dundas Street, also known as Highway 5, one of the earliest routes used by Ontario's settlers. Appointed Britain's first Secretary of State for War and the Colonies in 1794, Henry Dundas did rather well for himself generally, with Dundas County, Upper Canada; Dundas Island, British Columbia; Dundas, a suburb of Sydney, New South Wales; and Dundas Hills in Western Australia named in his honour.

His son, Robert, the 2nd Viscount, also fared well. As well as rising to be First Lord of the Admiralty twice from 1812, he was interested in polar exploration. It is thought that explorers to the area around North Star Bay in Greenland, later famous as the site of the Thule Air Base, the USA's most northerly military installation, chose Mount Dundas to recognise his interest. Dundas's enthusiasm for the Arctic is also remembered in Melville Sound and the vast Melville Island, the eighth-largest island in the Canadian Arctic. He is also honoured by another Melville Island, the second largest in Australia, off its Northern Territories.

Sir Archibald Campbell, lieutenant governor of New Brunswick from 1831 to 1837, had his moment of glory in the town of Campbellton, thanks to Robert Ferguson. After the Battle of the Restigouche of 1760, the last naval battle between France and Britain for the possession of North American lands, the victorious British encouraged settlers to occupy the newly acquired territory. There were many Scots among them, including Hugh Baillie, who in 1769 set up a fur and salted salmon business on the site of the future Campbellton. Eight Scottish fishermen were brought over from Aberdeen, two of whom provided their expertise of the salmon-fishing industry at Old Church Point. In the mid-1790s, Alexander and Robert Ferguson from Perth settled in Martin's Point, Robert becoming the largest merchant and fish exporter in Restigouche and its most important landowner. It was Robert who changed Old Church Point to Atholville after his native Perthshire and changed Martin's Point to Campbellton.

The exotic-sounding Campobello Island, New Brunswick, offshore from the most easterly town in the United States, reflects another Campbell and another governorship – Lord William Campbell, fourth son of the 4th Duke of Argyll and Governor of Nova Scotia from 1766 to 1773. Like many places, the island went through several name changes before settling with Campobello. It was originally known by its First Nation name, Ebaghuit, meaning 'lying parallel to the land'. The French fishermen who settled it in the early seventeenth century knew it as Ile des Coquilles. After the island passed to the British in 1713, it was gradually settled by New Englanders of Scottish and Irish descent. In 1765, Captain William Owen received a grant of 'the Outer Island, then called Passamaquoddy' from Lord William Campbell, Passamaquoddy being the name of the local First Nation tribe. Owen later wrote:

> I renamed the island Campobello, the latter partly complimentary and punning on the name of the Governor of the Province, Lord William Campbell, and partly as applicable to the nature of the soil and fine appearance of the island, Campobello in Spanish and Italian being, I presume, synonymous to the French Beau-Champ.

The Campbell in question was Lord William Campbell (*c.*1730–78), who, with no prospect of inherited income, opted for a career in the Royal Navy. In 1766, largely thanks to his family's influence at court, he was appointed Governor of Nova Scotia. Campbell went on to be appointed to his dream job of Governor of South Carolina, having married the daughter of one of the colony's principal planters. The American Revolution put paid to his title.

A century later wealthy American and Canadian city dwellers 'discovered' Campobello, one such holidaymaking family being the Roosevelts, including the infant Franklin Delano, future president of the USA. The Roosevelt Campobello International Park was established in 1964 following a gift of the Roosevelts' cottage and grounds jointly to the Canadian and United States governments.

Dalhousie, New Brunswick's most northerly town, repre-
sents another nod to a governor, in this case to George Ramsay,
9th Earl of Dalhousie and Governor-General of British North
America from 1820 to 1828. The loyal citizen who honoured
Ramsay was Captain John Hamilton of King's Cross near Whiting
Bay on Arran. Attracted by the lure of timber, Hamilton led a
party of Scots settlers to the area in the late 1820s. He opened
the first store, established a timber export business and was a
major benefactor of the Presbyterian Church. Having paid his
dues to the governor, he named nearby Inch Arran Point for
himself. He spent the last ten years of his life back in Scotland,
dying in Irvine in 1848. Three years later the grateful citizens erected a monument to Hamilton, commissioned from a
Glasgow firm.

Edinburgh-born George Robert Ainslie gave his name to
Lake Ainslie, Cape Breton Island. Through family influence, he
switched careers in 1812 from the army to colonial administration, firstly as Governor of Eustatius in the Leeward Islands, then
of Grenada and then Dominica. His hot-headedness and violence
in putting down a local uprising resulted in his being posted to
a rather less comfortable billet, as lieutenant governor of Cape
Breton. Liver disease, partial blindness and a drastic cut in pay did
nothing to enamour him of his new posting. He arrived to find
the local faction-ridden administration in disarray and the settlers
destitute. Many had come from the Hebrides, with Protestants
settling on the west side of the lake and Catholics on the east.
Ainslie's temper only exacerbated the situation. He dismissed
the islanders as poor illiterates and was secretly delighted when
the British government decided to re-annex the island to Nova
Scotia. He retired to lick his wounds and catalogue his collection
of coins, leaving little impression on the island other than the
name of a lake.

At the other end of the world the same pattern of naming places after scions of the ruling classes held. Born on the island of Ulva off Mull, Australian explorer, reformer and administrator Lachlan Macquarie had an immense influence in the transition of a penal colony to the heart of a future nation, as the 5th Governor of New South Wales from 1810 to 1821. He was the person who officially adopted the name Australia for the new country. The National Trust of Australia maintains his mausoleum at Gruline on Mull, where he chose to be buried. The memorial describes him as 'the Father of Australia', while many places in his adopted land remember him.

When he reached the Pacific coast in 1820 after exploring the interior of New South Wales, John Oxley called his arrival point Port Macquarie. Macquarie had instigated Oxley's exploration to identify new sites. Initially, the town was developed as a penal settlement. It was here that sugar cane was first grown in Australia, tended by a prisoner from the West Indies. Today, with a population of 40,000, Port Macquarie is famous as a beach resort and as 'koala capital of the world'.

Macquarie first visited Tasmania in 1811, his wife Elizabeth Campbell as always by his side. Tradition has it that he named Glenorchy, now part of metropolitan Hobart, after her homelands. Although she was born at Airds in Appin, the earliest Campbells of Glenorchy lived in a castle of that name on an island at the end of Loch Awe, Argyllshire. By 1864, the date of its becoming a municipality, Glenorchy boasted four churches, a school, a seminary, four hotels, a tannery and a jam factory: for a century to come, fruit growing was an important industry. Macquarie returned to Tasmania a decade later and on his travels stayed with David Gibson from Perth. He named a new settlement in northern Tasmania Perth after his host's home town. The land had originally been owned by Thomas Massey, described as a 'turbulent and troublesome man', but Massey moved to farm at Ellerslie near Ben Lomond to make room for the growth of Perth. Macquarie initiated a ferry across the South Esk River, with an inn and a military post. He paid homage to his wife Elizabeth Campbell in the Elizabeth River, which flows through Campbell Town, one of four garrison stations established between Hobart and Launceston.

Macquarie is one of the most celebrated Australians on the map, lending his name to Macquarie Island between Tasmania and Antarctica; the tectonic plate Macquarie Ridge; Lake Macquarie, the Macquarie River, the Macquarie Marshes, Mount Macquarie, once known as Mount Lachlan, the Lachlan River, the Macquarie Pass, Macquarie Fields, Macquarie Hill, even the Macquarie Rivulet, all in New South Wates; the Macquarie River, Tasmania; and Macquarie, a suburb of Canberra.

Other governors of the colony of New South Wales were not forgotten. The Hunter River and the Hunter Valley, New South Wales, are named after Leith-born John Hunter, naval officer, explorer, naturalist and second governor of the colony, from 1795 to 1800. Fellow Scot William Paterson from Montrose explored the region in 1801, naming its features after Hunter. Paterson was honoured in the name of a tributary of the Hunter River which he had also explored, the Paterson River. Thomas Brisbane, Governor of New South Wales from 1821 to 1825, gave his name not to somewhere in the colony but to Brisbane, the capital of Queensland since 1859, and to the Brisbane River on which the city stands.

Born in 1773 at Brisbane House outside Largs, he pursued a long and distinguished military career before being appointed governor by his friend the Duke of Wellington. Although his brief period in New South Wales was not easy due to rivalries and factions, he found the time to catalogue the stars of the southern hemisphere, the achievement for which he is best known today. In 1823 Brisbane instructed explorer and surveyor John Oxley to look for a site for a new penal colony for repeat offenders in Queensland. Oxley discovered the river which he called Brisbane and the next year chose a site for the colony at Edenglassie, where a bend in the river provided a natural barrier against escape. Edenglassie was named by chief justice George Forbes after the lands of the branch of the Forbes family in Banffshire – not a combination of Edinburgh and Glasgow, as is often claimed. Brisbane visited the new colony after spending a fortnight on storm-lashed seas. The convicts were set to work building their quarters and stockade. The colony was later renamed Brisbane in honour of the river and the governor. Free settlement only started in 1842, as the government wanted to keep the jail isolated from the wider community. Ex-convicts and entrepreneurs put down roots and by the 1880s Brisbane was the main commercial centre of Queensland.

The name Brisbane travelled as far as California's Guadalupe Valley. Developers originally envisaged the valley as housing some of the 250,000 people made homeless by the San Francisco Earthquake of 1906 in a new city to be called Visitacion. By 1929, when developer Arthur Annis arrived in town, Visitacion had a population of only 25. Amis's vision was to encourage people of limited means but reputable character to build their own homes, without unreasonable restrictions. He renamed his development Brisbane because he saw parallels with the pleasant landscape of the Australian city. Today, Brisbane has a population of 3,500.

Captain James Stirling, the first Governor of Western Australia from 1829 to 1838, is remembered in Stirling, now a residential suburb of Perth and the headquarters of the largest local government district of Western Australia. Born in Drumpellier, Lanarkshire, Stirling took up a career in the navy. In 1827 he travelled with botanist Charles Fraser from Blair Atholl, with a view to founding a settlement on the Swan River. The British government was keen to establish new outposts because of growing French interest in Australia and the need to create new penal colonies. In late 1828 Sir George Murray, the Colonial Secretary and an old family friend, appointed Stirling to lead a party of intending colonists. The next year, Stirling set sail as the lieutenant governor of Australia's first free colony. He marked out the site of the future state capital Perth, ten miles from the mouth of the Swan River. In naming the settlement, he followed the wishes of Sir George Murray, who was born in Perth and was its MP. In 1835, Stirling caught a glimpse of the range of mountains which his companion, Western Australia's first surveyor, John Septimus Roe, christened the Stirling Mountains. The colony's early years proved difficult: settlers were slow to attract and there were clashes with Aborigines, who used the Swan River to reach their coastal fishing grounds.

The tradition of naming places after governors lived on until the twentieth century. The suburbs of MacGregor, Brisbane and MacGregor in Canberra owe their names to Sir William MacGregor, Governor of Queensland from 1909 to 1914. Born on a farm at Towie, Aberdeenshire, he became a farm labourer until encouraged by the local minister, school master and doctor to complete his education with their financial support at Aberdeen Grammar School. On qualifying as a doctor and marrying his already pregnant wife in 1868, he opted for a career in the colonial service. He rapidly moved up the career ladder, becoming governor of Lagos and of Newfoundland before being appointed governor of Queensland and the first chancellor of Queensland University.

Having a place named for you was not exclusively the prerogative of governors, however. MacLeay Island, MacLeay River and Macleay Mountains all take the name of Alexander Macleay, the colonial secretary of New South Wales from 1825 to 1837. The island's original name, O'Shea's Island, has a more colourful origin. Tim O'Shea was an escaped convict who from 1837 lived alone among the mangroves for 14 years, never discovering that he had been pardoned.

Alexander Macleay (or MacLeay) was the son of the Provost of Wick. While working as a civil servant in London, he became fascinated by the study of natural history, amassing possibly the world's largest private collection of insects by 1825. He even had his own plant name, *MacLeaya cordata*, better known as the plume poppy. After being appointed colonial secretary of New South Wales, he arrived in Sydney with his wife, six daughters and his collection. He received several land grants, including Elizabeth Bay, overlooking Sydney Harbour, which he named after his wife. He built himself 'the finest house in the colony', with a garden that was 'a botanist's paradise'. In 1842, 500 leading colonists presented him with a silver candelabrum which his descendants presented to the New South Wales parliament. After his death his vast collection was transferred to the Macleay Museum at the University of Sydney.

Aberdeen, Dundas, Dalhousie – it helped to become a colonial supremo if you were already a scion of a Scottish aristocratic family. The hill station of Dalhousie is one of the few places in India not to have an Indian name. Like Shimla, it was created to serve as a summer retreat from the heat of the plains for British officers and administrators. Set in dramatic Alpine scenery, the town was centred around a sanatorium for convalescing British troops. Its buildings adopted European styles, including Scots Baronial. Sir Donald Friell McLeod, born in Fort William, Calcutta, of a military Scottish father in 1810 and future lieutenant-governor of the Punjab, named the hill station in 1854. He chose to honour the 1st Marquess of Dalhousie, born at Dalhousie Castle outside Edinburgh in 1812, who was serving as Governor General of India at the time.

The military men

Military leaders also had relatively high stakes in the place-naming game, especially if they died for it. Abercrombie, Nova Scotia, is a story of 'mights' as the family history is uncertain. Two miles upstream from the mouth of the East River, the settlement might be called after Scots-born General James Abercrombie, whose first commission may have been to fight on the government side at Culloden in 1746. An outspoken critic of his superiors, he had a somewhat chequered military career in Canada before dying at the Battle of Bunker Hill at the start of the American Revolution.

Now an eastern suburb of Pittsburgh, Braddock, Pennsylvania, was named after Edward Braddock, the town being built on the site of Braddocks Field, where he was wounded and defeated in battle. Born in Perthshire, Braddock was the son of an officer in the Coldstream Guards who secured a place for him in the regiment in 1710. As progress in his career was slow, in 1753 he changed regiment, briefly becoming acting governor of Gibraltar. The following year he was given command of an expedition to North America with the aim of putting the British colonies on a war footing against the French to push them back into Canada.

Braddock summed up the situation as his badly equipped, ill-disciplined troops faced a force of about 800, more than three-quarters of whom were Native Americans, the rest being French or Canadian: 'we are sent like sacrifices to the altar'. The ensuing battle on 7 July 1755 found Braddock's army helpless and confused, and Braddock himself shot in the chest, possibly by one of his own men. The army retreated, two-thirds of the men having been killed or wounded. A few days later Braddock surrendered his command and died, George Washington presiding at his burial service.

From the mid-nineteenth century, the town of Braddock looked to industry for prosperity, thereby acquiring a second Scottish association. Andrew Carnegie chose it as the location of his and America's first Bessemer steel plant. It was also the first place in North America to open a Carnegie library.

Sometimes it is the person who names rather than the name itself that provides the Scottish connection. The earliest reference to Pittsburgh is in a letter dated 27 November 1758, from Brigadier-General John Forbes to the British Prime Minister, William Pitt the Elder: 'I have used the freedom of giving your name to Fort Du Quesne, as I hope it was in some measure the being actuated by your spirits that now makes us masters of the place.'

Brought up in Dunfermline, Forbes opted for a military career, fighting with the government at Culloden. In 1757 he was appointed Commander of His Majesty's troops in the southern province of North America. He succeeded, where Braddock had failed, in achieving the French withdrawal from Fort Duquesne, a strategic site in the struggle between the French and the British for control of the fertile Ohio River valley. On hearing of Forbes' advance, the French set fire to Fort Duquesne and retreated. Mortally ill, Forbes renamed the fort after his patron Pitt. As a Scot, he would have intended Pittsburgh to rhyme with Edinburgh, where he was born. Pittsburgh remains one of the few US cities to be spelled with an 'h' at the end of 'burg'. For this reason, it is also the most commonly misspelled city in America.

Although the Otago area of New Zealand has many places named by homesick Scots settlers, Clyde is the exception. The town started life as a tented village to house some of the 40,000 gold diggers who moved in along the banks of the Clutha River during the gold rush of the mid-1860s. Some miners took up the option of buying title to the land. In 1865, the post office adopted the name Clyde – not after the river whose Gaelic name is Clutha but after the Glaswegian Colin Campbell, 1st Baron Clyde. He was the military leader in command of the Thin Red Line at the Battle of Balaclava in 1854 during the Crimean War and of British forces in India during the Indian Mutiny of 1857.

A recurring theme in place names associated with military men was the establishment of forts to protect British interests against potentially hostile neighbours. Grahamstown, Eastern Cape, South Africa, was founded in 1812 as a military outpost by Lieutenant-Colonel John Graham as part of the effort to secure the eastern frontier of British influence in Cape Colony against the Xhosa tribe, whose lands lay just to the east. Graham was born in Dundee into the landed family of the Grahams of Fintry. Taking up a military career in 1806, he was sent to South Africa to help Britain to re-occupy the Cape. Using 'a proper degree of terror', he forced the Xhosa to retreat and established Graham's Town as the region's central military post, linked to a string of forts along the Fish River. Grahamstown grew as farmers established themselves in more secure trades and emigrants from Britain were encouraged to join them. One settler in 1820 was the Scottish poet Thomas Pringle, who established South Africa's first newspaper.

Close to the Canadian border, Drummond Island, Michigan is the largest US island in the Great Lakes. Now a holiday resort, it once had a much more serious purpose. The British had established a fort at Mackinaw on Lake Huron during the American Wars of Independence. In the re-drawing of boundaries after the Anglo-American War of 1812, the fort of Mackinaw found itself in American territory. The British had to move their military outpost to a new location on what was then known as Manitoulin Island. From the start, they called it Drummond Island.

The Drummond the officers of the new fort chose to honour was Sir Gordon Drummond, the Quebec-born son of a Perthshire landowner who had emigrated in 1764 as the Quebec agent of the contractor victualling British troops in North America. He was educated in Britain, then chose a military career, playing a key role in the War of 1812. He briefly held the post of Governor General and Administrator of Canada before returning to Britain in 1816. The British abandoned the fort in 1828 after the joint commission to survey the boundary between the US and Canada decided that Drummond Island lay within US territory.

Even in the twentieth century Scottish military men are remembered. As its original name suggests, Pueblo Nuevo was a new town founded in 1954. For more than 30 years, it lacked road access to the rest of Chile. The authorities later decided to change the name of the community of just under 3,000 people to Cochrane. The 12,000-foot peak which dominates the neighbourhood is Cerro Cochrane and the stretch of water bordering Argentina and Chile is known as Lake Pueyrredón on the Argentinian side and Lake Cochrane on the Chilean side.

Every year naval personnel from throughout South America attend a commemoration service at the tomb of the founder of the Chilean and Peruvian navies in Westminster Abbey. The man they pay their respects to is Thomas Cochrane, 10th Earl of Dundonald, who was born in Hamilton in 1775. Cochrane's genius for seamanship ensured that he quickly rose through the naval ranks and covered himself in glory through the capture of French warships during the Napoleonic wars. Heaped with honours, in 1806 he successfully stood for Parliament. His fall from grace was equally dramatic. His hot temper led to what was in effect a conviction for libelling a superior officer. Worse was to come in 1814, when he was jailed for a year for his supposed involvement in a plot to defraud the London Stock Exchange by starting a rumour that Napoleon was dead.

Disgraced in Britain, in 1817 he accepted the invitation of the Chilean government to organise and command their fleet during their war of liberation from Spain. He went on to help to liberate Peru from the Spanish in 1820. Cochrane was now in great demand from countries seeking independence, including Greece and Brazil. In 1830, the accession of a naval monarch, William IV, and the end of 20 years of Tory rule allowed Cochrane to return to the fold of the British navy. Now 'a national treasure', Rear-Admiral Cochrane spent his last years writing his memoirs of an eventful and turbulent life.

Haigslea outside Brisbane, Queensland, was Kircheim until 1916. It was a farming community where over 60 per cent of householders had German names. During the First World War there was a reaction in Australia to places with German names and so the inhabitants decided to honour the Scotsman Douglas Haig, who was at the time Commander-in-Chief of the British Armies operating in France and Flanders.

Now a suburb of Adelaide, South Australia, Sauerbier became Aberfoyle Park for the same reason. German-born Christian Sauerbier had called into Scotland on his journey to settle south of Adelaide in 1845. He prospered and attracted other farmers to his land. After Christian's death, his son John Chris inherited the land and changed his name to Aberfoyle, possibly because his father may have lived in Aberfoyle, Perthshire, during his travels.

The cultural heroes

The world map of Scotland extends to places associated in real life with the creators of some of its cultural heroes.

Robert Louis Stevenson State Park, California, commemorates the place where the author spent his honeymoon in 1880, although nothing remains of the couple's cabin, an abandoned bunkhouse at the Silverado Mine. Stevenson published an account of his stay in *The Silverado Squatters.* Already in failing health, he had married American Fanny Vandegrift Osbourne somewhat against his parents' and friends' wishes. Although Stevenson's inspiration for his most famous novel, *Treasure Island*, is supposed to be Fidra on the Forth Estuary, east of his native Edinburgh, there is a real Treasure Island, an artificially created island in San Francisco Bay, built for the Golden Gates International Exposition of 1939. It once housed several fun fairs and a naval base.

In 1966 the Chilean government renamed two of the three islands in the Juan Fernández archipelago Alejandro Selkirk and Isla Róbinson Crusoe after the real life castaway on whom Daniel Defoe based his novel, *Robinson Crusoe.* Portuguese sailor Juan Fernandez discovered the mountainous, volcanic islands in 1575. They remained unknown other than as a refuge for pirates until Alexander Selkirk arrived.

The younger son of a shoemaker, Selkirk was born in Lower Largo, Fife, in 1676. Having fallen foul of the Kirk Session, he ran away to sea in 1693. In 1704, during a privateering voyage, Selkirk fell out with the commander over the boat's seaworthiness and decided to remain behind on the island of Juan Fernández, where the crew had landed to overhaul the worm-infested vessel. His possessions included a sea chest, clothes, bedding, a gun, a pound of gunpowder, a large quantity of bullets, a flint and steel, a few pounds of tobacco, a hatchet, a knife, a kettle, a Bible and other religious books, and his navigational instruments. He probably expected his stay to be no more than a few months but it was four long years before he was rescued.

An archaeological dig organised by the National Museum of Scotland in 2005 and contemporary accounts give some indication of his lifestyle. He built two huts, one as living quarters and one as a kitchen, near a stream for fresh water and a viewpoint from which he could scan the horizon for ships. He shot goats, eventually being able to outrun them, and used their hides for clothing. Plenty fruit and vegetables grew on the island, although ironically Selkirk did not like fish. He passed the time reading the Bible and singing psalms. During his stay, several ships passed by but only two, both of which were Spanish, came in to anchor. Selkirk was lucky to escape capture. By the time he was picked up by the Woodes-Rogers privateering expedition he was clad in goatskins and had difficulty stringing together sentences. Despite his adventure, Selkirk continued his life at sea, dying on board HMS *Weymouth* off Cape Coast, Ghana, in 1721, two years after the publication of *Robinson Crusoe*. It is not known whether the two men ever met, but Defoe undoubtedly knew of Selkirk's adventure.

Over time what must have been a harsh and lonely environment has become synonymous with an island paradise. Robinson Crusoe Island, Fiji is an upmarket beach resort boasting a blue lagoon, coral reefs, a long white sandy beach, palm trees, a traditional wood and thatched hut (*bure*), and friendly Pacific islanders.

WHO WAS ATOL?

One of the most unusual place names with a Scottish connection is Atolovo, a village in south-east Bulgaria. 'Atol' references John, the 8th Duke of Atholl, who provided financial support to create a settlement for Bulgarian refugees from Macedonia after the First World War. The village was built in 1926 under the auspices of the British charity Save the Children and has honoured the duke with a memorial. The duke has an even more unusual connection with Eastern Europe, being briefly considered as a candidate to become King of Albania in 1921.

8

A reminder of home

While many emigrants, especially from the Highlands, simply transported the name of their village or crofting township to a new setting in Canada or Australia, others chose to memorialise their homeland in more imaginative ways. Some celebrated the country itself and others with specific landmarks that reminded them of features back home. Particular views recalled the poetry of Burns or the novels of Sir Walter Scott. Even developers, who otherwise had no Scottish connections, capitalised on Scottish names, choosing them to convey the image they sought to project to prospective customers. Whimsy also played a part: among the more standard Scottish names in Newfoundland – Iona, Lochleven, Loch Lomond and Melrose – one stream is known as Tartan Lane River.

Some communities wished simply to stamp their settlement with a Scottish identity without naming names. Braeside in New York State, Glendale in California, Burnside in South Australia – especially in the mid-nineteenth century, romantic Scottish names were fashionable, whether or not the community had any specific Scottish associations. The USA has several variants of Mackville, some having modified their spelling over the years. Mackville, Michigan, was first settled by the McDowell and McDonald families. When the post office opened in 1898, the community was called McVille. McVille, North Dakota, is thought to have been founded by the McDougall family in 1906 after the arrival of the railway. Macville, Illinois, is now no more than a rusty sign and a cemetery, while MacVille, Minnesota, appears to have vanished completely from the map.

Scotland abroad

Southern Africa boasts not one but two towns with the name New Scotland, in Natal and Swaziland. Visionary, entrepreneur and eccentric, Alexander McCorkindale embraced the whole of his native land when he chose the name of his new ventures. The chilly, misty mornings and rolling hills of the high veld must have reminded the first settlers of home. In the early 1850s, McCorkindale, a Scots-born trader in animal pelts, had bought 200 farms from the government to establish an emigrant settlement in Natal. While negotiating the land deal and building a cottage for himself, he set up camp in a cave: his cave and cottage still survive. In 1856, he brought his wife, Mary-Ann, from Glasgow on the *Portia* with 80 emigrants, including 22 boys whom he had apprenticed from reform schools in Scotland.

The first New Scotland failed. Undaunted, McCorkindale negotiated a land deal with the King of Swaziland, promising a railway and a port in return. He upped sticks with 30 of the original settlers to a second 'Scottish Highlands transferred to wild Africa'. With the support of his friend, Marthinus Pretorius, President of the Transvaal, in 1864 he established the Glasgow and South African Commercial Agricultural and Mining Company for 'the settlement of able-bodied Scottish immigrants'. He declared the larger area to be the Republic of New Scotland, with Roburnia (later Amsterdam) as its capital in celebration of the Scottish bard. Attracting a second influx of around 60 Scots, McCorkindale constructed farm buildings of

Global Scotlands

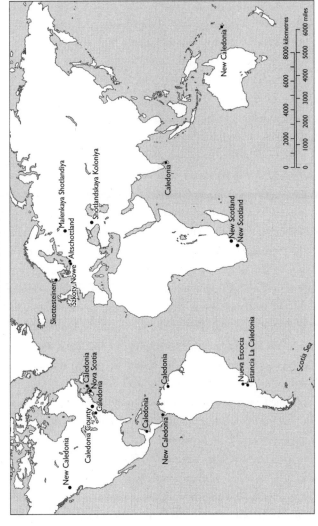

There have been global linguistic spins on the name 'Scotland' and 'Caledonia', the title that the Romans bestowed on the lands north of their frontier.

stone and thatch to look like their Scottish equivalents and gave the farms names such as Iona, Arthur's Seat, Waverley, Lochleven, Dundonald, Bonny Brae, Dumbarton and Craigerley. Many of these names survive today. McCorkindale planned to build a harbour on the coast and to deepen the Pongola River to allow ships to export goods from the farms. While investigating the route, however, he contracted malaria and died in 1872. It took two decades and a protracted court case to untangle his affairs. McCorkindale left a further legacy in the name of Miss Chrissies Lake. Childless themselves, he and his wife were very fond of President Pretorius's daughter, Chrissie. Lake Chrissie is the largest body of water in what's referred to as South Africa's 'Lake District'.

It was not only the promoters of the Darien scheme who opted for Caledonia, the name given to Scotland by the Romans. From Caledonia, New York State to Caledonia, Belize, reasons for selecting the name were legion. Captain James Cook, whose father was a Borders farm labourer, is one of the most famous explorers of all time, being the first European to make contact with the east coast of Australia and to circumnavigate New Zealand. On his three voyages, exploring and mapping largely uncharted territory, he faced the challenge of naming the coasts and islands which he passed. Coming up with thousands of names must have more than taxed his imagination. In 1774, during his second expedition, he sighted a south-west Pacific island. He named it New Caledonia because its north-eastern coast reminded him of Scotland. Contact by Europeans with the remote archipelago remained sporadic until Napoleon III annexed it as a French overseas dependency and penal colony in 1853.

On the same voyage Captain Cook also named a Pacific archipelago New Hebrides, a title that remained until the independent republic of Vanuatu was declared in 1980.

It is unusual to find Scottish references among the place names of Vermont, USA, redolent as they are of the leafy towns of the English Home Counties – Colchester, Reading and Windsor. Caledonia County in the north-east of the state is the exception. It was incorporated in 1792 a year after Vermont became the first new member to join the original 13 states of the Union. The name was adopted out of respect for the large number of Scottish emigrants who had purchased tracts of land in the area and established flourishing settlements in Barnet and Ryegate. By 1773, ten years after Ryegate had been named, Scots Presbyterian minister the Revd John Witherspoon owned most of the land. Born in Gifford in East Lothian, in 1768 he had accepted the invitation to become President of the Presbyterian College of New Jersey, the future Princeton University. He went on to become the only active cleric to sign the American Declaration of Independence.

Witherspoon had been approached by James Whitelaw and David Allen, agents for the Scots-American Company of Farmers in Renfrew and Lanark. This group from Lowland farming stock had appointed the two surveyors to look for land opportunities in America. After a lengthy search they decided on Ryegate. Whitelaw reported back: 'the ground here supports Indian corn and all kinds of English grain to perfection, likewise all garden vegetables in great plenty . . . Many things grow here in the open fields which the climate of Scotland will not produce such as melons, cucumbers, pumpkins and the like.' Among the town's many advantages was the fact that it was within six miles of 'a good Presbyterian meeting'.

By early 1774, settlers started to build homesteads and roads. The members later called the association the Inchinnan Company, partly because so many of them came from this area of Renfrewshire and partly to distinguish themselves from the similarly motivated Stirlingshire Company. The latter had purchased and settled a large tract in the township of Barnet, a little farther up the Connecticut River. These Scottish settlements formed the nucleus of Caledonia County, although few if any individual settlements adopted Scottish names.

Caledonia also lent its name to a very different environment, the rich coal seams of the Glace Bay area of Cape Breton Island. Although most mines were small scale and largely seasonally operated by the island's inhabitants as an additional source of income to crofting, as early as 1820 the General Mining Association was importing experienced colliers from Scotland and Ireland. Individual names reflect the Scottish influence. One of Canada's earliest railway lines was laid from the Albion Mines. It ran from Stellarton to a point near Granton on Pictou Harbour. In 1861, the Glace Bay Mining Company operated two mines, the Caledonia and the Stirling, while Port Caledonia was one of the rail trans-shipment points. The mining community of New Aberdeen took its name from John Campbell Gordon, 9th Baronet of Nova Scotia, 1st Marquis of Aberdeen and Governor General of Canada from 1893 to 1898. The booming collieries attracted immigrants from Scotland's mining communities. In 1911, if Cape Breton residents were not born in Nova Scotia, then they were most likely from Newfoundland, Scotland, Russia or Italy. Only a decade later the balance of ethnic origins had changed to Scottish, followed by English, Irish, then French.

The Caledonia mine is still remembered in a Cape Breton folk song:

When first I went to Caledonia
I got loading at Number Three
And I got boarding at Donald Norman's
He had a daughter could make good tea.

Scotland in song

Traditional Scottish ballads were transported across the Atlantic – and in the case of *Betsy Bell and Mary Gray*, all the way to Staunton, Virginia, via County Tyrone in Northern Ireland. On the way Betsy and Mary were transformed from 'twa bonnie lasses' into hills. The ballad tells of how Betsy Bell (or Bessie, as she is sometimes referred to) and Mary Gray fled from Perth to escape an outbreak of plague in 1645. The girls built a bower in the country and were supplied with food by a young man from the town who fell in love with them. He not only brought them food but also the plague and all three died. Scottish settlers in Northern Ireland's County Tyrone christened two mountains near Omagh after the two unfortunate lassies. Emigrants to America from Tyrone took the story with them. Behind the town of Staunton in the Shenandoah Valley there are two peaks, one called Betsy Bell and the other Mary Gray.

Poet Robert Burns collected and immortalised many Scottish ballads. Of all his works it is his own poem of 1791, 'Afton Water', which seems to have played on the heartstrings of homesick emigrants to the USA. Afton, New York, owes its existence to severe winter weather. The community was first settled in 1786 as part of the town of Jericho. A particularly violent storm during the winter of 1857 resulted in residents freezing to death or starving from lack of supplies. No help was forthcoming from the rest of the townspeople. When spring came, hard feelings resulted in Jericho splitting in two, becoming the new towns of Afton and Bainbridge. The local hardware-store owner, Joseph Chaffee, liked the Burns poem 'Afton Water' – and the fact that 'A' for Afton would be filed before 'B' for Bainbridge in state registers also appealed, as a way of cocking a snook at uncooperative neighbours. Unusually, there is also a village called Afton within the town of Afton.

The bard and the novelist – place names celebrating Burns and Scott

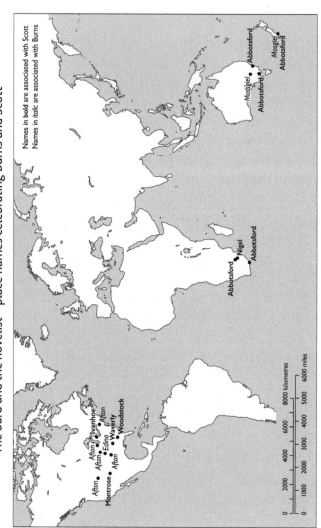

Names in **bold** are associated with Scott
Names in *italic* are associated with Burns

Afton *Afton* Ivanhoe
Montrose *Afton* *Afton*
Edina **Waverly**
Afton **Woodstock**

Abbotsford **Nigel** **Abbotsford**

Mossgiel **Abbotsford** *Mossgiel* **Abbotsford**

0   1000   2000   3000   4000   5000   6000 miles
0   2000   4000   6000   8000 kilometres

Scots took their culture with them as they travelled the globe, whether reflected in traditions such as Highland Games and tartan or in place names associated with their iconic writers, Robert Burns and Sir Walter Scott. The names celebrated the titles of favourite novels and songs, and homes associated with the two writers.

Afton, Iowa, acquired its name from romantic newlyweds Edward and June Temple. In 1854, the 23-year-old bank clerk had ambitions to build a new town and potential county seat. He and his business associates hoped to win over the authorities by offering half of the town's lots for public use, reaping their profits from the sale of the remaining acres. One sunny afternoon, after riding out for several days to prospect possible sites, Temple halted at a fine view, a ridge intersected by several ravines. He noticed that his wife looked distracted as she gazed over a gentle, meandering stream. He was prompted to quote the lines of Burns: '*Flow gently sweet Afton, disturb not her dream.*' Jane, a Burns enthusiast, responded: '*How lofty sweet Afton, thy neighboring hills . . . How pleasant thy banks and green valleys below.*' She thought that Afton would be a pretty name for the venture. Although Temple's new town never became the county seat, he did go on to found Iowa's largest insurance corporation.

Burns' poem had a similar effect on two railroad workers. Surveyor Anton Aires had already christened his daughter Afton because he liked the poem, so when a community sprang up in Oklahoma around the new Atlantic and Pacific Railroad tracks, heading towards Vinita in 1871, he named the settlement Afton. Another homesick railroad superintendent, Robert Harris, changed the name of the hamlet of Middleton to Afton, Wisconsin, when overseeing the arrival of the Beloit and Madison Railroad.

Scotland in words

Admirers of novelist Sir Walter Scott laid down literary connections wherever they went. Stephen Pavatt was one such fan of Scott's Waverley Novels, although his spelling was slightly off the mark. Stephen had already given his own surname to the hamlet, a stagecoach stop between Nashville and Memphis, Tennessee. When the site was chosen as the seat of the new Benton County in 1835, a more dignified name was in order, so Pavatts became Waverly, albeit dropping the final 'e'.

Petrus Marais, prospecting for gold in South Africa, happened to be reading the Sir Walter Scott novel *The Fortunes of Nigel* when he struck gold on the Varkensfontein farm in 1886. He immediately formed the Nigel Gold Mining Company. The town of Nigel sprang up around the mine. Nearly every street still carries the name of a character in Scott's novel, including Olifaunt Road, Moniplies Street, George Heriot Street, King James Circle, Dalgarno Street and Mungo Street.

Scots flocked to the largest and richest gold mines around the young city of Johannesburg, founded in 1886. Today the names of its suburbs still reflect the influence of those Scottish gold miners: Abbotsford (after Sir Walter's Borders home) Argyll, Balmoral, Birnam, Blairgowrie, Buccleuch, Craighall, Douglasdale, Dunkeld, Dunnottar, Dunvegan, Germiston, Glen Atholl, Glen Esk, Glenvarloch, Heriotdale, Kelvin, Melrose, Moffat View and Strathavon. Other Scott aficionados named Ivanhoe, Michigan, and Woodstock, Georgia.

The city and county of Montrose, Colorado, also owe their name to a Scott novel, *The Legend of Montrose*. Although settlers moved in during the 1870s, they could not legally purchase land until the Ute Indians had been removed to a reservation in Utah in 1881. The town was known by several names, including Pomona, Dad's Town and Uncompahgre Town, before Scott enthusiast and town founder Joseph Selig suggested the name Montrose to commemorate the hero of his favourite novel. The town prospered as a supply centre, first for mining and then agriculture, the world's longest irrigation tunnel opening in 1909 to bring water to the fruit farms.

There are Abbotsfords in Melbourne, Sydney, Dunedin, East London, Johannesburg, Philadelphia and British Columbia. References to Sir Walter Scott's home, however, can yield red herrings. Today, Abbotsford is the fifth-largest city in Canada's British Columbia. The city was named by a Scot but not in honour of Sir Walter. Young surveyor John Cunningham Maclure had come to British Columbia with the Royal Engineers, who were surveying the area in response to the Fraser River gold rush of 1858 and as part of Canada's assertion of its claim on British Columbia. The reward offered to the engineers after their tour of duty was the chance to buy land at a very reasonable price. In 1889 Maclure applied for a Crown grant for 160 acres of bush land – the future city of Abbotsford. He called his acquisition after his friend, Harry Abbott, the western superintendent of the Canadian Pacific Railway.

It was an English poet writing about a Scottish river who inspired a Scotsman and an American to name Yarrow Point, Washington State, a small town on a peninsula bordered on three sides by Lake Washington. In 1888, Leigh S.J. Hunt, owner of the *Seattle Post-Intelligencer*, became Yarrow Point's first land speculator. He built a large estate on the northern shoreline, which he named 'Yarrow' after a favourite poem by William Wordsworth.

In 1803, Wordsworth had spent time in the Borders and wrote *Yarrow Unvisited*:

> What's Yarrow but a river bare,
> That glides the dark hills under?
> There are a thousand such elsewhere
> As worthy of your wonder.

By 1814, after a journey down its length in the company of James Hogg, the Ettrick Shepherd, the poet felt more positively disposed to the river and revised his opinion in *Yarrow Revisited*:

> Flow on for ever, Yarrow Stream!
> Fulfil thy pensive duty,
> Well pleased that future Bards should chant
> For simple hearts thy beauty.

Which poem was Hunt's favourite is not recorded. Over time the name Yarrow extended to the whole peninsula. In 1907, Scotsman George F. Meacham filed the first development plan for Yarrow Point. He advertised lots for sale and sponsored a contest to name the streets, asking for Scottish suggestions. Sunnybrae, Bonneybrae and Loch Lane still appear on Yarrow Point street signs.

Bens and Glens

Mountains, lakes and glens often acquired Scottish names because features of the landscape not only reminded settlers of home but carried the image of Scotland to their new environment. Another Borders river plays a part in the history of Tweed, a village on the Moira River in central Eastern Ontario. In 1830, Allan Munroe dammed the river to erect the first saw mill. The settlement was initially known as Munroe's Mills and later Hungerford Mills. The operation changed hands several times until acquired by James Jamieson, a Scot who had traded his foundry business for the mills and surrounding land. He divided the land into village lots and named the place Tweed after the Scottish river in 1852. The mining, lumber and agricultural centre has two unusual later claims to fame. In 1967 Tweed residents elected what is believed to have been the first all-female council in Canada, albeit lasting only one term of office. In 1989 the Ottawa branch of the Elvis Sighting Society declared that Elvis Presley was alive and well and living in Tweed.

The name Tweed does not always have direct Scottish associations. The 50-mile-long Tweed River, New South Wales, flows from the Eastern Highlands to enter the Pacific Ocean at Tweed Heads. When English explorer and surveyor John Oxley visited the region in 1823, according to one of his companions, John Uniack: 'We also gave the name of Tweed to the river.' In turn the river gave its name to the coastal headland, a mountain range and a volcano. Today, like its Scottish counterpart, the Tweed also acts as a boundary, in this case between Queensland and New South Wales. The expression 'North of the Tweed' is used to refer to the people and places of Queensland; 'South of the Tweed' is used by Queenslanders to refer to the southern states of Australia.

Among the Bens, Ben Lomond was unsurprisingly a popular choice, especially among Australian settlers. There are several Ben Lomonds in New South Wales. Coming in all shapes and sizes, they include the Ben Lomond hills in Clarence Valley; a Ben Lomond between Gyra and Glen Innes where, when built, the railway was the highest in the southern hemisphere; a Ben Lomond in County Westmoreland; a Ben Lomond in the Liverpool Range; a Ben Lomond in Bathurst County; and a five-mile-long ridge named Ben Lomond in Wynyard County. The Ben Lomond range in Tasmania embraces the country's second-highest peak and the country's premier downhill ski slope. Explorer William Paterson named it after its Scottish counterpart in 1804. The naming was a close-run thing. Colonel Legge surveyed the area in detail a couple of years later, opting for historically significant names relating to the exploration of the Nile, governors, officials and fellow surveyors in Tasmania.

Emigrants often adopted the word 'glen' to give a settlement a Scottish flavour. From Glen Alice, New South Wales to Glenwoodville, Alberta, the prefix 'glen' conjured up pleasant images of misty hillsides and fast-flowing burns. There is a Glencoe in New South Wales and one in South Africa; a Glen Flora in Canada and the USA; and a Glenavon in Canada and South Africa. On the north shore of Long Island, Glen Cove, New York, is famous as a millionaire's playground. Its ten miles of waterfront was first settled by Native Americans, then seventeenth-century Europeans, and more recently by the millionaires who created 'the Gold Coast of Glen Cove'. Movie stars and baseball heroes took up residence among the families whose names were synonymous with wealth - Getty, Pratt, Woolworth and Kennedy.

The original name of the city had been Musketa Cove, from the Matinecock Indian 'this place of rushes'. Mills and clay-mining were the drivers of prosperity, the latter following the discovery by Scots-born doctor Thomas Garvie that the clay near his property, now called Garvie's Point, was of sufficient quality to make pottery. In 1827 he negotiated with Cornelius Vanderbilt to operate a regular steamboat service between Glen Cove and New York City. At first New Yorkers were reluctant to visit, mishearing or confusing the word 'Musketa' with 'mosquito'. At a public meeting in 1834 to discuss the need for a name-change, several possible options were debated. Local legend claims that someone suggested 'Glen Coe', which was misheard as 'Glen Cove'. The name-change was successful. By 1860 Glen Cove was a fashionable resort and by 1917 a fully fledged city.

Today, an affluent town in Du Page County, the name of Glen Ellyn, Illinois, also underwent several transformations. When frontiersman Deacon Winslow Churchill settled near here in 1834, a small village with a roadside inn, Stacy's Tavern, and a school house soon grew up. With the arrival of the Galena and Chicago Union Railroad in 1849, the focus of development shifted a mile and half to the south. Seizing the opportunity, Dr Lewey Q. Newton granted a right of way over his land and offered to build a depot and water tank at his own expense to persuade the railroad company to stop. The halt became known as Newton Station. Three years later, the new postmaster David Kelley declared, 'Since there is already a Newton, Illinois, the name should be changed to Danby – after my home town in Vermont.' So Newton became Danby.

The name changed again in 1874 to Prospect Park, possibly because the behaviour of a few local rowdies had besmirched Danby's image. In 1889 entrepreneurs Thomas E. Hill and Philo Stacy dammed the local stream to form Lake Glen Ellyn. They adopted a hybrid name reflecting the glen in which the lake is situated and the Welsh spelling of Hill's wife's name, Ellyn. The discovery of mineral springs and the opening of a brothel by Chicago's infamous Madam Rieck put the settlement on the map. By 1891, when it was advertising itself as Chicago's newest suburb and health resort, Glen Ellyn was finally adopted as the town's official name.

Twin cities

New settlements also adopted the names of Scottish towns and cities. Although known to otter fur traders, it was only in the mid-nineteenth century that the area around the future city of Aberdeen, Washington State, was settled. Samuel Benn, who moved here in 1868, recognised the trading potential of the area's natural resources of fish and lumber. With partners George Young and James Stewart, he opened the town's first cannery – the Aberdeen Packing Company – selling processed butter and meat to mining prospectors passing through town. In 1873, George W. Hume opened the first salmon canning factory.

In 1884, Benn submitted a plan for a town named Aberdeen. Early resident Jean Stewart told the story of its naming. 'I wrote a letter to one of the papers suggesting that the new settlement be called Aberdeen, since it was at the mouth of the Rivers Wishkah and Chehalis, just as Aberdeen in Scotland is at the mouth of the Don and the Dee, and also since Aberdeen means "at the mouth of the river". George Hume saw the letter, and when Mr Benn, in 1884, went to record the place as Heraville, he showed it to him and so the change was made to Aberdeen as being more appropriate.' A competing claim as to who christened Aberdeen came from engineer David Fleet, who argued that it took the name of his alma mater, the Aberdeen School for Boys, Virginia.

By 1890, Aberdeen boasted a population of 2,000, two sash-and-door factories, a shipyard, three salmon canneries, a hotel and two banks. Transport remained a problem until 1892, when the Northern Pacific Railroad offered to operate a line to Aberdeen provided the locals built it. Every able-bodied man donated ten days' labour in return for a plot of land, and local firms gifted the rails and ties. Completed in 1895, the railroad guaranteed Aberdeen's future status as a city by opening up markets for agricultural produce and timber: much of the wood used to rebuild San Francisco after the devastating 1906 fire was sourced from the area. In 1924, Aberdeen shipped its one-billionth foot of timber, earning it the title of 'Lumber Capital of the World'. Today the city is better known as 'the Birthplace of Grunge', as Kurt Cobain, singer-songwriter with Nirvana, was born in Aberdeen.

City names also appealed to property speculators. The development of Aberdeen, Massachusetts, now a residential suburb of Boston, began in earnest during the mid-1880s when a new electric trolley service arrived. Promoted as a 'Romantic Suburb' for wealthy commuters, the developers filled it with ornate houses in the Colonial, Georgian Revival, Queen Anne and Shingle styles. The upmarket homes were linked by a series of winding ways, respecting the natural contours of the rugged, wooded terrain. The streets still bear English and Scottish names, thought at the time to add to the allure and status of a residential area. In 1890 Aberdeen was advertised in the local newspaper as 'Several hundred feet above any considerable portion of land in the neighbourhood, commanding magnificent views in every direction, well-watered, a perfect combination of woodland, and glade, and admitting the free exercise of the artistic taste of the landscape gardener, these lands are sure to be sought for residential purposes by the most desirable buyers.' Aberdeen's growth was spectacular. Tired of living in dirty and crowded inner-city areas, well-to-do immigrant families were attracted by Aberdeen's bucolic image. The popularity of the car made commuting a viable option, and the expansion of the city continued. Aberdeen is now a designated architectural conservation area.

Inverness, Illinois, is the result of another Scottish property developer's dream. The story goes that in the mid-1920s Arthur T. McIntosh passed through this part of Cook County while searching for land where he could settle with his family. The area's rolling hills and lakes reminded him of Inverness. Another version is that McIntosh was a Chicago land developer who named his town after his clan's homeland. By 1926, McIntosh had purchased the first of 11 farms to provide the land for Inverness. He created a development that typified the traditional New England landscape, with roads that wound around the Inverness hills, only a few of which led into or out of the village. Every building lot covered an acre or more. McIntosh laid down rules for the new community – no fences or walls between lots, no kerbs and no streetlights to interfere with the landscape, which he planted with Norway pines. To ensure exclusivity and avoid ethnic diversity, he kept house prices sufficiently high to attract only the seriously wealthy. For many years, the McIntosh Company had complete control over the sale of lots, as well as the resale of homes. Incorporated in 1962, Inverness today is what Americans call a 'bedroom community' for Chicago. Half of the town's street names have Scottish connections, from Aberdour Lane to West Greenock Street, and for its golf-daft residents there is a Saint Andrews Lane and a Muirfield Drive.

Melrose, Massachusetts, eight miles north of Boston, was named Ponde Field when settled around 1630. It remained a scattered farming community until the arrival of the Boston and Maine Railroad in 1845, which attracted commuters keen to live the country life. Glasgow emigrant William Bogle set up as a wigmaker, making his fortune from a hair wash which he called Hyperion Fluid. He campaigned to change the town's name of North Malden to something more attractive. He advocated Melrose, it sounding pleasant and the area having a broken, hilly landscape which reminded him of the Borders. Two other civic leaders at the meeting in 1850, during which the name Melrose was adopted, also claimed to have put forward the name. Bogle's third reason was that this would be the first place in the USA to choose the name Melrose. Whether he was right or not, today there are at least 18 other locations with the same name, from abandoned villages to cities, from Connecticut to New Mexico.

The name Glasgow, too, has flourished. Glasgow, Kentucky, the county seat of Barren County, probably acquired its name from early Scottish settlers who moved here from Virginia at the end of the eighteenth century. Glasgow is proud of its roots, holding an annual Highland Games which attracts a crowd of around 20,000. Nearby is the Brigadoon State Nature Preserve,

181 acres of mature woods and farmland bordering the back-waters of the Barren River Reservoir. A previous landowner named the preserve after the mythical Scottish village which is supposed to appear from the mists every hundred years.

The battling Scots

Two of the most famous battles fought on Scottish soil have won their place in the world atlas, the first by design and the second through a misunderstanding. Although the first settlers to the affluent North Shore area of Bannockburn, Illinois, were from County Meath in Ireland, it was Scottish architect and builder William Aitken who created the modern town from 1924. His masterplan was to build 'country estates' for people like the members of his bridge and country clubs, who wanted a genteel style of living. Aitken called his own home 'Bannockburn' and the name came to encompass the whole community. Five years after the town was established, 30 families had moved in. Residents were very active in shaping the community that they loved, serving as trustees on the village board, organising the Bannockburn school, creating zoning rules to ensure that Aitken's vision remained intact, running a garden club and raising money for charity. To keep taxes low, facilities such as a police station and a community hall were slow to develop. The Tri-State Tollway was built through the village in the 1950s, encouraging commuter growth. Despite this, much of Aitken's garden suburb concept has been retained, including his name in Aitken Drive.

It is often assumed that Culloden, Georgia, commemorates the last battle on British soil, when government forces quelled the Jacobite uprising under Prince Charles Edward Stuart in 1746. In fact, Monroe County's oldest town is named after not the battle but its Scottish founder, William Culloden, who settled in the area in 1780 after service in the British navy and a trip to an uncle who had an indigo plantation in India. Having abandoned his initial plan to grow tobacco, he opened a store and post office on land that was to become the future village. Initially known as Lebanon, the settlement was renamed Cullodenville in 1821, a decade before its founder's death. The 'ville' was dropped when the town was incorporated in 1887. Today, Culloden is rediscovering its Scottish roots, with a Highland Games and an annual Homecoming.

More Scottish than the Scots

Many overseas communities outdo Scotland in the way that they celebrate their roots today. Glen Innes, New South Wales, describes itself as 'the Celtic Capital of Australia'. High in the New England Tableland, this is Beardie country. Distinguished by their long, flowing beards, the first stockmen in the area, escaped convicts John Duval and William Chandler, roamed the vast plains in the 1830s. They guided Glen Innes' first settler, Leith-born lawyer Archibald Boyd, to the district. Boyd had emigrated in 1838 and took up 'Boyd's Plains' and two other properties. Ruined in the 1840s depression, he returned to Britain to lobby for settlers' rights and write romantic fiction with titles like *The Duchess: or Woman's Love and Woman's Hate*.

Glen Innes takes its name – as does Thrumster, New South Wales – from Archibald Clunes Innes and his Caithness birthplace. Innes was largely responsible for transforming Port Macquarie from a penal settlement to a flourishing town. He arrived in Sydney as captain of the guard in the convict ship *Eliza* in 1822. After several years chasing escaped convicts in Tasmania, he became commandant of the penal settlement at Port Macquarie in 1826. Following a sojourn in Sydney, he returned as police magistrate and was granted 2,568 acres of land and contracts to supply the penal colony with food. Using convict labour, he transformed the wilderness into Lake Innes, for many years the greatest pastoral property north of Sydney. He acquired sheep and cattle stations all over northern New South Wales, three of which were later named Innestown, Innes Creek and Glen Innes. At his height, one of the wealthiest and most hospitable men in the colony, Innes, like Archibald Boyd, lost his fortune in the 1840s and became bankrupt in 1852.

The route from sheep station to Celtic Capital reflected Scottish pride. To mark Australia's Bicentenary in 1988, the Celtic Council of Australia proposed a national monument to honour the nation's Celtic pioneers – the Scots, the Irish, the Welsh, the Cornish and the Bretons. Glen Innes won the competition with a proposal for the Australian Standing Stones, inspired by the Ring of Brodgar in Orkney. Completed four years later, the Standing Stones has become an iconic meeting place for people and clans with Celtic connections throughout Australia.

If there was a competition for the world's most Scottish community, Maclean, New South Wales, would be a strong contender. It describes itself as 'the Wee Scottish Town in Australia' and as 'Australia's First Scottish Town'. For over a century, the Lower Clarence Scottish Association has hosted the Maclean Highland Gathering each Easter weekend, when the town's population of 3,000 more than doubles. The town's calendar is peppered with Scottish events – the Kirkin' of the Tartan in April, Tartan Day in July and Scottish Week in November. A nod to other immigrant cultures is made with the Lower Clarence Dance Eisteddfod in May. Street names, many of which are bilingual in Gaelic and English, include McLachlan Street, Argyle Street, Oban Lane and McIntyre's Lane. The town boasts Australia's oldest Free Presbyterian Church, which still administers to the spiritual needs of the descendants of early settlers. A local park features a Scottish cairn constructed from rocks from around Australia and Scotland to mark the town's bicentenary. Some telegraph poles have even been painted tartan.

The obsession with all things Scottish is intriguing, given that the origin of the name is quite prosaic. It is thought that escaped convict Richard Craig reported finding a big river fringed by timber forests in 1832. He later worked for a Thomas Small of Sydney, who was sufficiently inspired by Craig's reports to send his brother and two dozen sawyers to investigate the 'Big River'. The party camped on the future site of Maclean on the Clarence River. The surveyor planning the settlement named it after the surveyor-general of New South Wales, Alexander Grant McLean, who had emigrated in 1837 when his father was appointed principal superintendent of convicts. Many of the first settlers were Highlanders, who moved from the Hunter Valley.

The most romantic of all Scottish images is perhaps Gretna Green. On the west bank of the Mississippi, Gretna, Louisiana, was originally an early nineteenth-century settlement known as Mechanicham. A local justice established its reputation for 'no questions asked' quickie marriages. After the village merged with neighbouring McDonoghville in 1913, it was natural to call the new community Gretna. The local museum has a blacksmith's shop, where Valentine weddings are conducted.

Sometimes romance was almost accidental. With access to iron ore, timber and limestone Mount Gretna, Pennsylvania, developed a smelting industry from the 1740s. Robert Habersham Coleman, the great-grandson of one of the early ironmasters, promoted the construction of a railroad from Lebanon to Cornwall in 1883. He headed a committee to select station stops along the line. Advised by their surveyor, who identified a spot about three miles west of Cornwall as 'a place thickly wooded, seemingly a road to mountain solitude', the committee decided to site a recreation area and station there. When one member, Hugh Maxwell, told his wife of the decision that evening, she suggested the name Gretna. The committee then appended 'Mount' to give it added appeal. In 1884, Coleman created a recreation park around the new Mount Gretna station and dammed a creek to create Lake Conewago. On his invitation it became the summer camp for the Pennsylvania National Guard, the United Brethren and the Pennsylvania Chautauqua, an educational family summer camp movement popular in the US until the 1920s. The park included a hotel and a Hall of Philosophy. Other developers, including the operator of an amusement park, moved in. From Memorial Day to Labor Day, the summer resort was packed with holidaymakers, including honeymooners. After the Second World War, the village gradually changed to a year-round residential area.

Its border location between the USA and Canada inspired the name of Gretna, Manitoba. Its original name, Smuggler's Point, reflected the village's rationale, as dense tree cover helped to conceal illegal border trade. When the 49th parallel was established as the international dividing line, Gretna became an important customs centre for both governments, as well as a trans-shipment point for grain. According to tradition John, the son of the settlement's founder, Stirlingshire tenant farmer William Ogilvie, named it Gretna after the border village in Scotland.

Some Gretnas were chosen simply because Scots associated with their development liked the name. Today, the motto of Gretna, Florida, is 'small city, big heart'. It was founded by a Mr Umphrey, who moved from Scotland County, North Carolina, to help set up a turpentine mill. As some early settlers had Scottish connections, the name Gretna was chosen for the new community. Gretna, Nebraska, was founded in 1886 on land along the new Burlington Northern Railroad line. The reason for its name is now lost, the assumption being that Gretna was chosen as many early residents had Scottish roots.

Although the actual name of Aberdeen, Ohio, was chosen to honour Aberdonian Matthew Campbell, its first settler around 1788, the activities of two residents forged the link with its current boast as 'the Gretna Green of America'. In the 1800s, these two 'squires of Old Aberdeen, Ohio' married thousands of couples without requiring a licence. Many of these marriages, later validated by an Act of the State Legislature, were between runaway slaves who had crossed the Ohio River from Kentucky on the underground railroad. Today, the town's 'Welcome' sign boasts of it being home of the Annual Gretna Green Festival.

The powerful image of Scotland still captures the imagination. Recently, two property developers adopted the name Malenkaya Shotlandiya, or Little Scotland, for their low-rise suburb on the northern outskirts of Moscow. They chose it to play on Russian enthusiasm for all things Scottish, from whisky to Burns. They also felt that promoting the Scots virtues of courage and canniness would appeal to potential buyers of the thousands of two-storey townhouses, which were significantly cheaper than most property in central Moscow. The town's logo is a Scottie terrier sporting a tartan tam-o'-shanter.

The 'e' in McKenzie Towne, a suburb of Calgary gives the game away that this is a recent development. The settlement was masterminded in 1984, and in the mid-1990s the artificial McKenzie Lake was created as a focus for leisure and further development. In 2002 the Urban Land Institute gave the town the accolade of being one of the top 26 contemporary communities in the world. Already with a population of more than 16,000, it is divided into three residential areas – Elgin, Inverness and Prestwick – each with its distinctive architectural style.

RECALLING SCOTLAND IN THE TRENCHES

Some of the most poignant memories of home on the map are the features of the battlefields of the First World War. The Lochnagar mine crater at La Boiselle on the Somme, the largest man-made mine crater created on the Western Front, took its name from the adjacent trench, Lochnagar Street. In the summer of 1915, the 7th Gordons were deputed to dig trenches round the village. Many soldiers came from Deeside in Aberdeenshire: they included workers from the royal estate at Balmoral, overlooked by the peak of Lochnagar. An officer went round naming the La Boiselle trenches after local landmarks in towns such as Perth: Scone Street, Tay Street, Inch Street and Fairmaid Street became the addresses of soldiers destined to die on the first day of the Battle of the Somme, heralded by the eruption of the mine which created the Lochnagar crater.

Index of Scottish place names

Africa

Aberdeen Island, Sierra Leone 178–9

Aberdeen, South Africa 136

Alexander Bay, South Africa 3–4

Blantyre, Malawi 126, 139

Blythswood, South Africa 138, 166

Campbell, South Africa 135–6

Chrissie's Lake, South Africa 200

Dumbarton, Rwanda 140–1

Dundee, South Africa 75

Edina, Liberia 141

Fraserburg, South Africa 136

Glencoe, South Africa 75

Gordon Memorial Mission, South Africa 138–9

Grahamstown, South Africa 111, 191

Johannesburg (suburbs), South Africa xi, 206

Livingstone, Zambia 3, 139

Livingstonia, Malawi 139

Lovedale, South Africa 138

Mac Mac Falls, South Africa 74–5

McGregor, South Africa 137

Melsetter, Zimbabwe 111–12

Murchison Falls, Uganda 171

New Scotland, South Africa (Natal) 198

New Scotland, South Africa (Swaziland) 198

Nigel, South Africa 206

Orkney, South Africa 74

Pirie, South Africa 141

Robertson, South Africa 136–7

Roburnia, South Africa 198

Sutherland, South Africa 137–8

Victoria Falls, Zimbabwe/ Zambia 2–3

Antarctica

Abernethy Flats 34–5

Beardmore Glacier 38

Caird Coast 39

Cap du Challenger, Kerguelen Islands 45

Cape Dundas, South Orkney Islands 43

Coats Land 35, 37

Dundee Island 43–4

Arctic

Australia

Index